Blueprint To Your Foreclosure Fortunes

Renegade Real Estate Riches

Written By
Timothy Johnson

LEGAL NOTICES

Published by Nomad CEO Publishing

Table of Contents

FORWARD

It is common knowledge that buying a home is one of the best investments you can ever make, but there is a way to reap even bigger rewards in addition to the normal benefits of homeownership by purchasing a foreclosure bargain.

If you have been sitting on the fence wondering if you should buy now or wait a little longer, then the fact that banks, real estate agents and motivated sellers are selling foreclosure bargains for pennies on the dollar should have you salivating with excitement. In fact, the current state of the real estate market that we find ourselves in is the perfect storm for investors. However, taking advantage of this market comes with one requirement: You must take action *now*.

No more stalling, no more procrastination, no more day-dreaming about what it will feel like once you have your own private little get-away. No longer can you straddle the fence, waiting and hoping that something better comes along. See, you are guaranteed to miss out if you are trying to time the market to find rock bottom bargains.

What you hold in your hands is the ultimate step-by-step blueprint to take you by the hand and guide you through the danger-riddled, but rewarding journey of buying a foreclosure *today*.

Introducing The "Foreclosure Bargain Buyer Program (F.B.B.P.)"

The Foreclosure Bargain Buyer Program (F.B.B.P.) is a proven system of buying a foreclosure home anywhere. This unique program hands you the keys to unlock every vital tool, little-known resource and hidden piece of knowledge about buying your first foreclosure *before* you begin buying. F.B.B.P. breaks the foreclosure home buying process down into manageable sections, which answers your most pressing questions about buying a home.

By the way, just so you have no doubt, this book *is* the foreclosure bargain buyer program. What you hold in your hands is the direct result of hundreds and thousands of hours spent over the years. This program was compiled as I was performing face-to-face interviews and consequently advising homebuyers from all types of income levels, races, creed and backgrounds. What I have done for you is to condense the best, smartest and most efficient way to buy a foreclosure home. This is an easy to follow guide that will literally change your life for the better.

Who needs this book? You do, if you are buying a home and you are:

- ✓ A first-time homebuyer who realizes that you want and desperately need answers to your questions before buying your first home.

- ✓ A newlywed couple eager to start your family, gain your freedom and establish your new lives together.

- ✓ A divorced or unmarried mother needing security and safety for your family as well as a fresh start.

- ✓ A single person refusing to wait until you are married to make one of the best investments. Heck, buying a house makes you even more attractive.

What "The Foreclosure Bargain Buyer Program (F.B.B.P.)" Will Do For You

Simply put, this book will give you solutions to your most troubling real estate questions, save you a boatload of money and help you avoid costly mistakes. But more importantly, within the pages of this book I reveal a simple to follow advice which allows you to gain access to years of insider real estate secrets, tips and strategies, while buying your foreclosure home. What you hold in your hands are the exact answers to questions you may have, but most likely do not even realize you will need answers to until well into your foreclosure buying process.

However, keep in mind that what I am revealing within these pages is my personal and exclusive foreclosure buying program for my personal clients. I use this unique system to advise my clients on how to find and lock-in the best deals for foreclosure bargains while walking them step-by-step through every phase of the home buying process. You now have access to this system 24/7 from the comfort of your own living room.

By investing in this book, you opened the door to an entire library of information about investing in foreclosures that will serve as guiding lights of inspiration, encouragement and sometimes an occasional slap on the wrist. Use this information, as it will provide valuable support on your journey.

Now, keep reading, then go buy your dream home.

Timothy Johnson

CHAPTER 1

Cashing In On the Foreclosure Crisis NOW

For many, many years now I have been speaking with dozens of real estate investors, helping thousands of families discover the joy of homeownership, and uncovering piles of down payment cash. I can say I have pretty much heard every confidence draining question there is, such as: "What if I lose my job?" or "Am I too young?", or my favorite "I can't find anything in the price range that we are pre-qualified to buy."

My many years of helping homebuyers find answers to those questions means that I am uniquely qualified to give you a simple yet effective way to blast right past those excuses. After reading this book, you will know with 100% confidence that right now is probably the best time for you to invest in foreclosures. Now, let me give you some information about the unique benefits of buying a foreclosure bargain and owning a home in this economy.

Why Buying Your Foreclosure Bargain Home In Today's Economy Still Makes Good Sense

Here is a little pop quiz to get us started. Do you know how many homeowners lost their home in foreclosure because of the reported 300+ or more mortgage lenders going out of business from 2006 to early 2011? Well, if you watched the news and listened to the media, you would think the answer is hundreds of thousands, or possibly millions of homeowners lost their homes due to lenders going belly-up. However, the real answer is None. Zero. Zilch.

"Not one homeowner lost their home due to the mortgage industry collapse."

Most people incorrectly assume that the mortgage debacle caused homeowners to go into foreclosure and lose their homes, but it is actually the other way around. Homeowners, who for any number of reasons, were unable to make their monthly mortgage payment greatly contributed to the mortgage collapse. The reason why homeowners did not go into foreclosure because of the mortgage industry collapse is because *their mortgages were insured.* Every person who lost their home to foreclosure during the mortgage collapse was simply unable to make their monthly payment because of rising mortgage payments, loss of their job or some other misfortune. The fact of the matter is, if those homeowners had the money to make the payment, they would still be in their home today.

It is this unfortunate abundance of folks who lost their homes which provides tremendous opportunity for you today. There hasn't been a golden opportunity like this in a very long time. You could probably spend another twenty or thirty years waiting for the same window of profit potential that we have now.

When you get down to the nuts and bolts of how you can invest in foreclosures during these economic times, it comes down to these facts; you must buy homes at a bargain price that you can continue to afford even in a worst-case scenario. You must use a fixed interest rate mortgage that never increases, while squirreling away enough emergency money for a rainy day fund.

Regardless of all the pressure to keep paying rent until the market gets better, there is still no doubt that investing in foreclosures today provides great tax advantages. It is also still true that owning your own home allows you to build wealth while providing security and stability for your family. Regardless of what the market is doing, those benefits do not change. They are truly timeless.

The Benefits Package Foreclosure Bargain Buyers Enjoy

When you feel those brand new house keys in your hand and hear that little soft jingle in your pocket after buying your home, you will feel like a brand new person with a renewed passion for life. There are few joys in life that come as close, and there are some very good reasons why you should feel so good. Investing in foreclosures gives you access to wealth by building equity when you or your tenants make your mortgage payments, while having something tangible that you own to show for it, and is the gateway to a multitude of tax breaks.

> **Example:** Mary stumbled across a good deal when she bought her first home. Her manager told her about a home on his street that he'd watched slip into foreclosure over the past several months and eventually was listed on the market for sale. She ended up buying her house for $185,000 when it was actually appraised for $215,000. She pays $1,250 per month towards principal.

> Principal Amount = $185,000
> Market Value = $215,000
> Equity = $30,000 ($215,000 - $185,000)

The Best Thing Since Sliced Bread....Almost

As you make your monthly payment and begin living your new life, you slowly begin to accrue something called home equity – simply by making your payment. Equity is the difference between what you owe on your home and the market value. Building equity means that as you pay your mortgage, the principal amount (the total amount you borrowed) of the loan decreases and the home value could go up. Many people have been able to retire and live a comfortable life because their home built up so much equity over the course of their lives. And as a result they then sold their home, took the money and launched their own successful business. However, before you begin seeing dollar signs, I must also warn you that sometimes the home values decrease for any number of reasons. But do not worry about that too much because according to the National Association of Realtors, home prices have increased an average of 6.5% each year for the last fifteen years.

Goodbye Landlord….Hello Home!

I am convinced there is no better feeling in the world than telling your landlord that you are moving into your new house next month so he or she will not be able to fund their retirement plan with your hard-earned dollars.

This feeling alone is truly priceless.

Seeing Where Your Money Is Going

One of the many joys of homeownership is that each and every month you actually get to touch, feel, see and smell your money. This means that you can actually track where your money is going and it forces you to save money each month by paying your mortgage payment and building equity.

This is a forced savings plan which provides a roof over your head.

It's All Yours!

The first several months of waking up in your new home will flood your mind with a flurry of emotions. The thought most often shared by new homeowners is the overwhelming feeling of, *"Is this all mine?"*

You Finally Catch A Tax Break

Everyone dreads paying taxes, but when you are renting, you have a higher level of dread when April 15th rolls around. Well, when you own a home you might actually begin to look forward to tax time because you begin to hear that old familiar cash register cha-ching sound.

Here is why: You get to deduct your mortgage interest, as well as many other items such as:

Homeowner Tax Deductions	
Points	Home Equity Loan Interest
Private Mortgage Insurance	Property Taxes
Interest on Home Improvement Loans	Home Office Expenses
Prepayment Penalties	Moving Costs

Having these additional deductions means thousands of dollars in tax savings for you each and every year. Pretty sweet, huh?

As if that was not enough, when you sell your home after living in it for two of the last five years, you do not have to pay taxes on the first $250,000 of profit that you make when you sell your home. But wait, it gets better. For those of us who have joined our lives together in holy matrimony, we get to keep $500,000 tax free.

Thanks Uncle Sam.

The Top 11 Excuses You May Be Tempted To Use To Procrastinate From Buying Your Foreclosure Bargain NOW...

Since I call planet Earth my home, I know sometimes in life we all get a little discouraged or overwhelmed with large financial decisions. So, in an attempt to help you out, I will provide answers to some of the major excuses you might begin to tell yourself to stop from investing in a foreclosure bargain, and the few times you might absolutely be right in doing so:

Excuse #1: "I Can't Afford A Home..."

When you say you cannot afford a home, what you really should be saying is that "I cannot afford a home that costs $400,000, but I *can* afford a home that costs $225,000." You can use this fill in the blank formula whenever this mood overcomes you. It quickly snaps you back into the reality that it is about the size of the mortgage you can afford.

When it comes to affording a home you should always remember it is as easy as adjusting the mortgage amount and maybe taking a little longer to save for a down payment.

Excuse # 2: "I Don't Have Enough Money For The Down Payment."

When I hear this excuse I automatically know it usually means the house the buyer really wants requires more of a down payment than they currently have. It is also important to keep an open mind and seriously consider downsizing to the amount of down payment you can afford. Within the pages of this book are many answers to the problems of not having enough money for a down payment, so be prepared to get off that bus pretty quickly!

Excuse # 3: "I am Afraid To Buy Because The Economy Is Bad."

While it is true that the economy is not bustling with activity, thousands of people just like you are preparing to make their best move. After all, these are the very same circumstances which cause "buyers markets." A buyers market simply means that there are more houses for sale on the market than there are available buyers who can purchase them. As a result, home sellers are more willing to be flexible with price, terms and extras in order to get their homes sold.

Your number one goal in a bad economy is to buy smart, insure yourself, your home and your income and make sure you have substantial savings in the bank before AND after you purchase your home. Buying your foreclosure bargain this way will help ease any fear you have of the market doing a nose dive once you move into your new home.

Excuse # 4: "I do not know what to buy…I'm confused."

This is a common concern for many foreclosure seekers, so let me give you several ways to get clarity quickly. The first tip is to follow your gut and listen to your instincts. If you are constantly drawn to condo's because of little to no maintenance, then think of the reasons why you feel this way and go with it. You *should* be looking for condo foreclosures. Do not try to convince yourself to buy a raised ranch with a huge backyard, which requires ongoing maintenance.

The next tip is to keep an open mind while visiting a variety of properties. This will allow you to narrow down what you do not like and will give you the confidence to recognize what you do like, instead of second guessing yourself. I don't mean to get philosophical on you, but follow these two steps and you will begin to see a clear path where there was only confusion before.

Excuse #5: "I Actually Enjoy Renting..."

Now, you might be one of the few people who actually enjoy making your landlord wealthy while you sweat and toil for every penny. If that is you, put the book down and slowly back away before I jump through the pages and put you in a headlock until you yell "Uncle!"

However, if you are like the rest of us, then you enjoy the luxury of keeping more money in your own pocket and the freedom of not stressing about where you live. Those luxuries and freedoms are virtually nonexistent when you are renting. By renting, you will always be paying someone else for the right to have the illusion of living a life of luxury and freedom, but at the end of the day you know deep down in your heart your landlord is the one really calling the shots.

Excuse #6: "But I Don't Know Anything About Home Maintenance Or Home Repairs."

Well, join the club. There are millions of folks who flock to Home Depots across the nation each weekend to take classes on plumbing, painting and gardening. Additionally, some of the most popular television shows are based on fixing up, repairing and improving your home. Get ready to become an expert user of Tivo for more recording reruns of old Friends episodes. Investing in foreclosures is more like a journey than a destination. You will have plenty of time and practice to become the handyman, or handywoman, you've always wanted to be.

Excuse #7: "...But What If I Lose My Job?"

Unless you are planning on buying your house for cash, then you must join the millions of hardworking Americans who manage to keep a job and pay their bills. If you are that concerned about losing your job, then I would strongly advise you to find a career and job in which you can feel more secure.

We both know that you will always have to maintain some form of income to support yourself and your family, regardless if you buy a home or not. So, why not have something to show for all those years of working your butt off? Additionally, you should really take some time to learn about disability, unemployment and mortgage insurance coverage in case of financial disasters.

Excuse #8: "It is Way Too Much Responsibility..."

Can you remember when you first learned to drive? Remember worrying about cars in front of you...cars in back of you...keeping your hands on the wheel...and watching the rear view mirrors?

The first time you do anything you will be threatened with fears of feeling overwhelmed, but do not give in to those fears. The financial obligations of making your monthly payment are the same as when you are renting. You pay or you do not get to stay, regardless if you are renting or owning. The difference is in the painting, mowing and managing the repair guys when you need work done.

Don't sweat it. It ain't rocket science, you can do it.

Excuse #9: "I'll Wait Until I am Married..."

Over the years I have seen a number of couples who opted to buy a house together before getting married. I personally would recommend that you take some time out for some serious thought before going this route. Why? Because I have seen a number of couples who break up after they have bought a home together and then they have to go through a mini-divorce before ever actually getting married.

However, do not misunderstand what I am saying here. There is no good reason why you should wait for Mr. or Mrs. Right to come along before you begin getting all the great benefits of homeownership. Get started today. My advice is that you should be looking for a smaller home and consequently a smaller mortgage if you are going at it alone.

Yes, I know there is a chance of meeting Mr. or Mrs. Perfect five minutes before your closing, but if he or she really is "the one" for you then he or she will recognize your potential by watching you handle the responsibility of homeownership.

Trust me when I tell you that owning a home is a feather in your cap to a prospective spouse.

Excuse #10: "I Feel Like I am Taking Advantage of People."

There are many folks who share this belief because they do not truly understand what is going on when a person is in foreclosure. In fact, by the time you are putting in an offer for a bank-owned foreclosure home the previous owners have already vacated the house and it is already owned by the bank. There is no little old lady or young family to evict from the house because the bank has already taken back possession of the house. In actuality, when you purchase a foreclosure you are contributing to helping the economy get back on track and helping property values increase.

Excuse #10: "This Pep Talk Is Great…But I am Still Scared"

Let me be the first to tell you this in case you have not heard it before. It is very likely **YOU WILL BE SCARED THE ENTIRE**

TIME! There…it is out of the way. I am not going to try and do a Jedi-mind trick on you and tell you that you should not be afraid. It would not matter anyway because you would still be scared. The fact of the matter is EVERYONE is shaking in their boots when buying their first foreclosure bargain, but you can minimize the fear when you have the knowledge, tools, resources and a great real estate team supporting you.

That is what this book is all about: Giving you the knowledge, tools, resources and showing you how to pick a world-class team of real estate experts to guide you through the best and biggest financial decision of your life.

On The Other Hand, Renting May Be Your Best Option If…

- **Renting may be your best option if…you are moving cross-country within months.** If your ideal dream of living the good life is hauling your entire life back and forth cross country several times a year, then owning a home may hold you back from your dream life.
- **Renting may be your best option if…your income will be dramatically less soon.** However, you may still be able to afford a smaller home or condo, but you should wait until your new level of income is determined.
- **Renting may be your best option if…your credit needs a lot of work.** Having two of three credit scores above 640 is a necessary requirement in this new real estate market. If you are not there yet, then you need to get the help of a professional to assist you.
- **Renting may be your best option if…owning a home costs you three times what rents costs in your area.** There are some parts of the county where you really have to be a millionaire to buy a home. In this case you have two choices: continue to make the rich even richer by paying rent or buy in a different town or neighborhood.
- **Renting may be your best option if…you need to have options.** If you spend half the year in Italy and the other half

in Spain then you only need a hotel room when you are in town to repack for the next move. You most likely do not need a 2,500 square foot raised ranch in Kalamazoo.

- **Renting may be your best option if...you honestly do not have two nickels to rub together.** There are always costs to be paid out of pocket for the appraisal, home inspection, etc. For example, when you moved into your apartment you needed a two or three month security deposit. Well, investing in foreclosures is an even bigger decision than renting an apartment, so you also need to have *at least* two to three months of mortgage payments.

Blueprint To Your Foreclosure Fortunes

CHAPTER 2

Don't Listen To Those Late Night Infomercials!

Within the last several years I have heard and seen countless so-called real estate experts give horrible advice to foreclosure homebuyers. While some of the advice is slightly true, the way in which they instruct buyers to go about buying their foreclosure home may not always apply to buying in your town.

For example, almost every single foreclosure buying book makes buying a foreclosure or bank-owned property seem as easy as a walk in the park. It could not be further from the truth. Sure, you can certainly make the journey easier if you have the guidance of an expert to walk you through it, but even with the help of the experts, there is still some risk involved. So here are my top eight reasons to ditch the late night TV way of buying a foreclosure and embrace the legal, safe but still profitable method of buying a foreclosure bargain:

8 Reasons Why You Should NOT Buy Your First Home Following The Advice Of A Late Night TV Salesman

Reason #1 - The late night TV way ...leaves you clueless on the exact steps of the foreclosure home buying process.

Have you ever been watching a scary movie and the music gets all creepy and the main star is just about ready to peek around the corner? You want to yell at the television screen because the person does not see the nastiest, ugliest alien monster to ever walk the face of the Earth getting ready to eat them alive. That is how it can be sometimes when you are buying a foreclosure home without knowing what you are doing. You do not even see what is about to go wrong next, but you have a sneaky suspicion that something's up.

The problem is that when you are buying your first foreclosure bargain, you do not have a reference point to compare things to. If you just go with the flow, then you will constantly be in limbo about what to expect next. There is no worse feeling than not knowing what is happening or where you are in the process. You need to have a step-by-step guide throughout your entire foreclosure buying process.

Reason #2 – The late night TV way...gives you information from five, ten or twenty years ago, which is outdated, generic and canned. Buying a foreclosure bargain home in Miami Beach, Fl today is NOT the same as buying a foreclosure in Dallas, Texas.

I am a big supporter of using the Internet and scouring bookstores for information on buying your foreclosure bargain. In fact, I strongly recommend it. However, you should know that much of the information you will read in most real estate books will NOT apply to buying a foreclosure home in your town.

The most common mistake I see in most resources is that they do not give readers the benefit of knowing that there are really three different times that you can buy a home during foreclosure. However, only one of them is advisable if you want to get a home in good condition. The three times are: Before foreclosure, during foreclosure and after the bank has taken back the property at auction. By the way, the best time to buy for most 'newbies' is after the bank has bought the property back, because most times they do the repair work to get it back in decent condition.

To buy your first home you need current, relevant and specific information about buying in your desired location.

Reason #3 – The late night TV way ...does not consider that everyone does not have ten, twenty or fifty thousand dollars just lying around the house.

Have you ever noticed how the real estate experts casually throw around the expression "five, ten or twenty percent down" like it is nothing? Well once you do the math on the purchase amount you will quickly see that five, ten or twenty percent of $320,000 equals $16,000, $30,000 or $65,000.

For the average hard-working person it could take five or ten years to save up that kind of money, but in the meantime you lose $50,000 or $60,000 because over the same period of time you are paying that much in rental payments!

Reason #4 - The late night TV way ...does not recognize that the housing market in your town has a mind of its own and requires special expertise.

In case no one has offered up this piece of information yet, let me be the first to tell you: Preparing an offer and negotiating for a foreclosure bargain home all require different strategies and techniques which cannot simply be lumped together into one.

Additionally, based on my years of experience, I have noticed that there is even a better way to find the bargain deals in certain neighborhoods than in others. These are just a few of the many little details which require the services and expertise of a local expert.

Reason #5 – The late night TV way...lies to you and tells you that it is easy to make money hand over fist buying foreclosures with bad credit, no job and no income.

Unless you are working with an investor, if you are even *thinking* about buying a foreclosure bargain you need AT LEAST: Three to six months worth of cash savings, a 650 middle fico score, a steady line of employment for two years or more and a team comprised of a real estate agent, loan officer, appraiser, home inspector and a real estate attorney. Do not let anyone set you up for failure or worse…foreclosure.

Reason #6 - The late night TV way ...does not take into account that the mortgage programs available change frequently and vary dramatically.

Did you know that each state, town and city can offer different mortgage programs for buying foreclosure deals, which are all based

---

on different criteria? Many books I read talk about buying foreclosure homes with mortgage programs that do not even exist in certain areas. I cannot even begin to tell you how many times I have received questions from homebuyers in Richmond, Virginia about mortgage programs which only apply for some neighborhood down in Raleigh, North Carolina.

In order for you to get the best deal possible on your foreclosure you need to know your options at the state, city and neighborhood level.

Reason #7 – The late night TV way …dangerously assumes that most real estate professionals truly want to take the time to educate you, the buyer, on every step of the process.

When it comes to purchasing foreclosure bargains, what you don't know can absolutely hurt you. Sadly, all you have to do is watch the evening news or search online for a couple of minutes to discover that something went wrong. At some point some real estate professionals stopped properly educating their clients in order to make a quick buck. You should always feel comfortable asking your real estate agent or loan officer any question you desire, but in reality you will most likely learn that you have a two or three question per phone call maximum.

Now do not misunderstand me: There are many hard-working real estate agents and loan officers making an honest living. However, there are many shady real estate folks who keep you in the dark about crucial information so they can pad their bank accounts.

Reason #8 – The late night TV way …assumes that you know how to negotiate with your real estate agent, loan officer, appraiser, home inspector, home insurance agent and everyone else in the process.

Do you know what to politely yet firmly say to a real estate agent to open up a conversation about commission fees if the seller does not pay the home buying fee? What about your level of effectiveness in talking to your loan officer about the amount of points, fees and interest rates on your mortgage? If your answer is no to those two questions, then how will you learn what to say in order to stop from losing tens of thousands of dollars out of your pocket? Not to worry, because I will reveal the answers to those questions in a few minutes within the pages of this guide.

The ONLY Way To Buy Your Foreclosure Bargain Home 100% Hassle-Free, Make A Profit And Virtually Eliminate Your Stress

The one and only way you should make the biggest financial decision of your life is by being armed with local real estate knowledge and a team of honest, **expert, local** real estate professionals. Notice the emphasis on local and expert. I cannot tell you how many horror stories I have heard over the years of foreclosure homebuyers who mistakenly placed their faith in a voice on the other end of the phone who is probably eight hundred miles away and who can never be found if there is a problem. On the other end of the spectrum, I have seen the first-time foreclosure buyers who entrust their most important financial decision to a newbie real estate agent two days out of real estate school.

Now before you think I am a mean person, let me state that I firmly believe in supporting professionals who are just starting in their profession, but I also believe in having experienced and expert advice when it comes to my money. How about you?

You must make certain that you have answers to your questions well before you start signing legally binding contracts. Why in the world would you start signing forms, documents and making agreements before you know exactly what to expect next? What you need in order to choose a foreclosure home in good condition in the ideal neighborhood at a bargain price is a comprehensive resource specializing in your desired location.

And that is what you hold in your hands.

CHAPTER 3

What You Need To Know Before You Even *Think* About Buying A Foreclosure

After helping hundreds of bargain buyers over the years, I have seen every twist, turn and hiccup that you could imagine. Sometimes it is a pleasant surprise, but most times it is an emergency fire, which has to be put out. So, that gives me a unique perspective on what foreclosure buyers should know before spending one dollar to buy a home.

What Are Foreclosures?

There are some basics that we need to cover first before I send you galloping off into the sunset with your moneybags. The first basic concept that you need to grasp is the whole idea of foreclosure. When I mention the word foreclosure, most investors instantly think that means buying the homes while the homeowners are unable to make their payment on their home and are forced to watch helplessly as their homes are sold at an auction.

While this may be true in some cases, there are three main stages that make up a foreclosure; pre-foreclosure, public auction and post auction.

For the purposes of this book I will most often be referring to post-auction foreclosure investing, because I believe that the average homebuyer has a better chance of success by focusing on these two areas. Now, that is not to say that you cannot have success purchasing at auctions or investing in pre-foreclosures. It has just been my experience that those two techniques require much more expertise than the average homebuyer currently has. In order to better illustrate this point, I will discuss the three main methods of investing in foreclosures, so that you will know exactly what your options are.

While researching foreclosure investing, you will also come across the terms short sale, bank-owned and REO. So, here are some quick and easy definitions so that you will be prepared.

- **Short Sale** – The home seller's lender agrees to accept less than what is owed on the property, but they consider the mortgage paid in full.

- **Bank-Owned & REO (Real Estate Owned)** – Homes that have been repossessed by the bank because they did not sell at the auction.

The 9 Steps of The Foreclosure Process

In order for you to have the best chance of buying a foreclosure, I will cover the steps of the foreclosure process. This way you will understand exactly where the homeowner is in the process, and then you will have a good understanding of the right strategy to maximize your profit potential:

1. *Homeowner misses a payment:* This happens for any number of reasons, but once it starts, it snowballs and it becomes hard for the homeowner to get caught up.

2. *Lender sends a payment reminder:* Lenders usually take the high road at this point and assume that the homeowner forgot to make their payment. Lenders usually send a reminder notice within 15 days.

3. *Lender does not receive payment:* Lenders will then send out another series of letters. They will also follow up with several phone calls to see why the payment hasn't been made.

4. *Lender sends account to internal collections:* At this point the account is approaching 60 - 90 days late and the lender turns over the account from regular billing to their own internal collections department. This is most often referred to as the 'loss mitigation department.'

5. *Lender hires attorney to file a Summons and Complaint and/or a Lis Pendens with the local courts:* Once the account reaches 90 - 120 days the account is turned over to an attorney who is hired by the lender to try to collect the money. However, the attorney also files a Summons and Complaint and/or a Lis Pendens. This basically lets the courts know that the lender has not received payment and wants the homeowner to come to court and explain what is going on or they will foreclose on the property.

Loan work out: If the attorney can actually get the homeowners on the phone then he will try to negotiate a temporary solution to get the homeowner caught up on their payments. This is sometimes called a loan modification or work out. This can be a good option for the homeowner if they can prove that they can get back on their feet in a short amount of time.

6. *Homeowner or the court decides on strict foreclosure or foreclosure by sale and sets a court date:* If the homeowner does not answer the Summons and Complaint, then the court will decide if the foreclosure will be a strict or a foreclosure by sale. The court will also set a day that they will issue a judgment.

Strict Foreclosure – If the homeowner or courts decide on strict foreclosure, then a "law day" or series of law dates are set in which the homeowners have to pay or be evicted. There is no sale with strict foreclosures. The homeowner loses their home on the date the court decides.

Foreclosure By Sale – The traditional foreclosure auction.

7. *Posting the property:* Assuming that a foreclosure by sale is taking place, then the county marshal's office will post a notice of foreclosure on the home and inspect the house. If the house looks abandoned the courts may expedite the process. Even at this point the homeowner can still make the

back payments, late fees and costs and bring the mortgage current. There are also notices posted in local newspapers or legal news of the town or city.

8. *Bid adjustment*: One day before the public foreclosure auction, the bank will adjust the opening bid to reflect the exact amount of the mortgage balance, fees, penalties and costs.

9. *Auction day*: This is the day that the courts actually sell the house to the highest bidder. This is usually a very low-key process, except of course for the homeowner who has to be out of their property that day or shortly thereafter.

The Three Basic Types of Foreclosure Investing

No matter how many different creative techniques you read or hear about to invest in foreclosures, all techniques are centered on buying foreclosures in one of three stages:

1. **Pre-foreclosure** – Purchasing the foreclosure while the owner is behind by one or more months. This may involve negotiating with the lenders in some cases.

2. **Auction Buying** – This is the traditional foreclosure auction. This is when several bidders either submit an offer to buy the property to a court appointed trustee, or openly bids in an auction type setting.

3. **Post Auction (Bank-Owned Properties)** - These are also known as repossessed homes that the banks have taken back from the owners. These are usually in decent condition or have substantial discounts because of damage.

The 3 Golden Laws of Investing In Foreclosures

While buying foreclosures is a highly profitable investing strategy, there are three laws, which if violated, can lead to a huge disaster for you. In fact, I am fairly sure that ignoring these laws accounts for eighty to ninety percent of the reasons why investors lose tens of thousands of dollars when buying foreclosures.

Here are the three golden laws of foreclosure investing.

- **Rule #1 - NEVER buy a foreclosure that is in a bad location**: Even if the banks or owners are giving the home away, do not accept it. It is not worth worrying about your house being robbed, burned or in a total inaccessible location. The worst part is that you will probably never be able to sell the home and make a profit because of those same reasons you should not have bought the property in the first place.

- **Rule #2 - NEVER buy a foreclosure that has bad design**: I could spend the next twenty pages telling you about bad design, but the rule of thumb here is to follow your gut, because some rules are not meant to be broken. (Yes, the following are designs that actually exist.)

  Examples:

  - No front entrance to the house.
  - You and neighbors share the same driveway
  - The only bathroom is in the finished basement

- **Rule #3 - NEVER buy a foreclosure that has bad construction**: This one may be tougher to catch on your own, but you can easily get a home inspector to let you know the truth. You are looking for things like foundation issues, wood that is rotting away that should not be, or a "supposedly" brand new roof that leaks.

How To Prepare An Offer On Your Foreclosure

Once you decide on your specific foreclosure investing strategy, your next move is to find a potential property, and then prepare a bid. However, before you submit a bid for any property, there are three steps you should always make. Secondly, there are some differences in how you prepare a bid, depending on the condition of the home. Generally speaking there are four types of property conditions you will uncover:

1. **Vacant and accessible:** In this case you are able to go inside the house and look at everything. This is the ideal situation because you can get all the facts without being interrupted.

2. **Occupied and accessible:** In this case someone currently lives there, but you are also able to go in and do a full inspection at-will.

3. **Vacant and inaccessible:** This is when no one lives in the house and you cannot get inside the house to do a full inspection. This is one of the worst positions to be in because you do not have all the facts you need in order to make an informed decision.

4. **Occupied and inaccessible:** When you find a property in this condition, it usually means the current occupants or tenants are not very friendly. You should really proceed with caution in this situation.

Once you determine the condition of a prospective home, there will always be at least four additional steps you must take. The three mandatory steps are:

1. **Get an estimate of how much it will cost to repair the property.** The best way to get an estimate of repairs is to have a licensed contractor visit the premises and review the work you want to have completed.

2. **Get an estimate of what the property value will be after repairs are made.** An appraiser and real estate agent will be

able to give you an estimate of how much the value of a property will increase once repairs are completed.

3. **Get an estimate of how much your costs will be to purchase the property.** This includes your mortgage payments, insurance costs, repair costs and every cost associated with purchasing the property.

4. **Calculate your maximum bid limit based on your personal finances and your goals for the property.** Unless there are some special circumstances, you should never bid above the market value in repaired condition minus your costs to purchase the property.

Bid-Calculating Worksheet

Opening Bid Amount	**$250,000**
Estimated After Repair Market Value	**$320,000**
Anticipated Monthly Rental Income	**$2,200**
Expenses	
Estimated Insurance	$1,500
Estimated Loan	
Estimated Loan Cost	
Property Document Cost	
Utility Expenses	$2,500
Repair Costs	$15,000
Eviction Costs	
Unpaid Taxes	

Anticipated Rent Loss	
Other Expenses	
Total Expenses	$19,000
Estimated Market Value	**$320,000**
Deduct Expenses	**- ($19,000)**
Amount to bid for Break-even price	**$301,000**

For example, if a property would be worth $350,000 after you make $50,000 in repairs, you should not bid above $300,000 for the property. In a best case scenario you would want to bid at about 75% of the after repair value:

Example:

$350,000 x 75% = $262,500

23 Foreclosure Bargain Buying Quick Insider Tips

1. Not every foreclosure is a golden opportunity for you.

2. Foreclosures are everywhere, but if you are just starting to invest in real estate, you only want to buy a foreclosure near your job or current home. (Investment property rule)

3. Gas is expensive and time is precious; do your research before driving around looking at properties.

4. Use the Internet as often as possible to research properties.

5. Don't confuse charity work with making a bad business deal.

6. Only buy properties you know how to manage and want to manage.

7. Managing a multi-family home is a 24/7 job.

8. Know the market for selling before you buy.

9. Only buy properties that you want to own for a long time.

10. Anyone losing their home is very unlikely to paint and clean the carpets on the way out.

11. Realize the different times during the foreclosure process in which you can buy.

12. When it is easy to buy, it is often hard to sell.

13. Bankers become more conservative as more homes go into foreclosure.

14. Fixer-Uppers normally cost more and take longer to fix than you think.

15. Not all houses are worth more than they cost to build.

16. A foreclosure may not wipe out all debts from the title.

17. The IRS may have a right of redemption period.

18. If a home seller is in bankruptcy, then the process can drag out much longer.

19. You can actually help the seller by buying their house.

20. When the market is soft, like now, it is better to buy and hold than to buy with the goal of flipping for a quick profit.

21. Buy within 20 minutes of where you currently live.

22. Making a good deal on foreclosures takes knowledge and patience.

CHAPTER 4

Strategy #1:
Buying Pre-Foreclosures Before The Auction

With the recent downswing of the market, pre-foreclosure investing has taken center stage. Many first time homebuyers and investors have taken their shot at buying homes from distressed sellers. However, there is a right and wrong way to invest in pre-foreclosures. Doing it the right way leaves you with a clean conscience and huge profits, but doing it the wrong way can cost you years of legal fees and ironically, turn you into a distressed seller.

The Benefits of Buying During the Pre-foreclosure Stage

If you want to have the greatest chance to make the biggest profit, then buying pre-foreclosures offers the best opportunity. While I personally do not think investing in pre-foreclosures is for every investor, if you have the resources and ability to negotiate with homeowners and manage a team of contractors for needed repairs, pre-foreclosure investing may just be for you.

Here are several of the major benefits of investing your time and money into buying pre-foreclosures:

1. You are buying the properties directly from the owners. There are no third-party people to go through, such as real estate brokers or government agencies.

2. You can reap huge rewards by buying the owners equity directly at a steep discount.

3. You get the chance to thoroughly inspect the property and estimate accurate property repairs.

4. You get to skip the auction process, which can be overwhelming and intimidating for some people.

3 Ways You Rescue A Distressed Pre-foreclosure Seller

Many times the media portrays foreclosure investors as predators preying on people during their time of weakness; however, my years of experience have shown me otherwise. Sure, you have the scum who take advantage of people, but the large majority of investors are good, honest folks who are simply looking for a deal.

The other side of the coin is the homeowner themselves. Usually by the time the foreclosure is looming, they are at their wits end and have tried any and all solutions. So, by the time an investor like you makes a decent offer, they are jumping for joy. Here are the main three ways that the homeowner benefits when you buy their pre-foreclosure:

1. **Homeowners possibly make some money on the sale.** When you negotiate a good bargain for yourself, you are also allowing them to walk away with some money after closing. This would never happen if they were foreclosed upon. So, even if it is only five thousand dollars, that amount is found money to the sellers.

2. **You save their credit from reflecting a foreclosure on their record.** One of the biggest challenges for homeowners after they have gone through a foreclosure is the process of rebuilding their credit. So, if they are able to avoid showing a foreclosure on their credit, then you are putting them ahead of the curve when it comes to fixing their credit.

3. **You allow them to have some dignity and save face.** Being forced to move from your home is a tough pill to swallow; however, doing it with signs all over your front yard that say "Foreclosure Sale" is even harder to go through. When a homeowner is able to sell their house privately, they are able to avoid an embarrassing situation.

A Day In The Life Of A Distressed Seller

One of the most important realizations you need to keep in mind when considering pre-foreclosures, is the mindset of the homeowners. Most times they are being forced to sell their home because of divorce, illness, loss of spousal income or just plain mismanagement of their finances. Regardless of the reason, it is a sensitive time in their life and they are very emotional.

So, as you consider this foreclosure buying strategy, you need to be very considerate of the folks who you will be contacting and negotiating with.

The 9 Steps of Investing In Pre-Foreclosures

Now we will take a closer look at the 9 steps which are involved in investing in pre-foreclosures:

Step 1: Get Your Mortgage Lined Up

The first step for you is to get pre-approved for a mortgage. Getting pre-approved first allows you to know how much you qualify for. You also need to make sure you have your down payment money readily available. Getting pre-approved first will put you in the right frame of mind and will make sure that you are financially prepared to invest.

This is a simple first step, but many people avoid it. I have come across many investors over the years that mistakenly thought the financing would "magically" fall into place once they found a bargain. Do not make the same mistake they did. Get pre-qualified first.

Step 2: Write Down Your Goals, Needs & Wants For a Foreclosure Bargain

Once you have been pre-approved for a mortgage, your next step is to match up your likes, dislikes and goals with what you can actually afford. So, you will need to make a written list of things that you cannot live without, or things you can. For example, if having a front and backyard to have your family over for barbecues and family events is important to you, then it needs to be at the top of your list. At the end of the day, you should know your priorities before you begin, because you will definitely see homes which have things you would have never even considered.

Step 3: Find A Pre-foreclosure Bargain

This is one of the most important steps in the process, because if you cannot find a bargain that makes you money, then you do not have a deal. Fortunately, locating homeowners who are several months behind on their payments and are knocking on the door of foreclosure is not too difficult to find in our current real estate market.

There are several ways to find these types of bargains, so here are my proven methods.

1. Checking the newspapers for upcoming foreclosure sales known as legal notices. Contact those owners directly and see if they're interested in selling their home.

2. Asking local real estate agents who specialize in foreclosure sales. You can find these agents by checking the home seller's magazines for the distressed seller listings.

3. Subscribe to an online foreclosure list service, which sends you targeted foreclosure listings matching your needs in your area.

4. Sign-up for a service which sends you a list of homeowners who are sixty to ninety days late on their mortgage.

5. Post classified ads in your local newspapers looking for distressed homes to buy.

Sample Ad:

Trouble Making House Payments
Call 203-123-4567 Today For Help

***When you select a service to provide you with leads, be sure to purchase or find at least 50 to 100 potential deals. Chances are that many will be working on other options besides selling to an investor at a steep discount.

Step 4: How To Contact Distressed Homeowners

According to many pre-foreclosure investors, the toughest part of investing with this strategy is contacting the homeowner in a way that does not offend them or make them angry. If you do not have a thick skin, then pre-foreclosure investing might not be for you.

Now, before I go any further I must warn you that there is only one way to contact distressed homeowners. The best non-offensive way to contact distressed homeowners is by mailing a series of 6 – 12 letters over an 8-week period.

Here is why I highly suggest direct mail:

1. **Using direct mail is easy.** You do not have to worry about making phone calls to anyone. You just mail out your letters and wait for a call back from interested prospects.

2. **Mailing letters is as cheap as it gets.** You can probably mail out about 100 letters at a time for about $70. This will allow you to get your message in front of a lot of potential bargains with little money out of pocket.

3. **Mailing the letters is relatively quick.** Most times sellers will respond within a week or two if they are interested. That means you can expect a pretty fast turnaround time with your potential bargains.

4. **Direct mail is efficient and effective.** You can reach hundreds of people at a time. All you have to do is spend a little time putting the letters in the envelope and you can potentially get your message in front of your ideal seller.

Rules to follow when using direct mail
- Target your letters using zip codes because that will help you focus on profitable bargains in good areas.
- Hire a professional copywriter to write the letters.
- If you are writing the letters, you want to focus on: Debt relief, cash for their equity, relief from foreclosure, avoiding a foreclosure on their credit reports and help in finding another place to live.
- Type the letters and personally sign them.
- Send them first class using a postage stamp.
- Send at least 6 – 12 letters at regular intervals.
- DO NOT make cold calls to homeowners in foreclosure.
- DO NOT make door-to-door calls to homeowners in foreclosure.
- Always repeat the same message in your letters:
  - I want to buy your house today.
  - I will be able to close within 30 – 60 days.
  - I will handle the details of the sale of your house.
  - I will help you find another place to live.

Questions to ask prospective home sellers
- When did you make your last payment?
- How much do you owe your lender total, including late fees, interest and legal costs?
- Do you have any outstanding judgment liens?
- Have you filed for bankruptcy in the last 24 – 36 months?
- Has your lender started foreclosing on your home?
- How much equity do you think you have left in your property?
- When would be a good time for us to get together to further discuss helping you out?

***Do not make an offer on the property at this stage. You do not have near enough the information to make an informed, intelligent decision about an offer price.

Step 5: Meet With The Seller And Get All Details About The Defaulting Loan

Once you have a prospective bargain, your next order of business is to get all of the relevant information about the mortgage. When you are meeting with the homeowner, be sure to emphasize that you cannot prepare a proper offer until you have all the information about the current mortgage and title unless you have a signed borrower's authorization form. So, you will need to do two things:

1. Meet with the home seller and get as much verifiable information about the mortgage and title as possible. The best way to do this is to use a worksheet that guarantees that you ask all the right questions.

2. Get a borrower's authorization form signed by the homeowner or get them to give you a payoff order, which lets you know how much they currently owe up to a specific date.

Step 6: Hire A Real Estate Attorney

After you have received all of the relevant information from the property owner, you need to immediately hire an experienced real estate attorney to write up a contract.

Many novice investors will skip this step and try to perform the title search and write up the contract themselves. Do not make the same mistake that most first time investors make. Order a complete title search from a local attorney on the property so you know all existing liens and stakeholders for the property. Title searches can cost you anywhere from $200 - $500.

More importantly, when it comes to writing up a legal purchase and sales agreement, hiring an attorney will pay for itself many times over in protecting yourself and your investment.

Step 7: Determine the home value

Now, if you want to get an accurate idea of the value of a home, then you must get an appraisal performed on the home. Although you can get an estimated range of the market value of the property by having a drive-by appraisal performed or having a real estate agent perform a comparative market analysis (CMA), you will want a complete appraisal done at some point.

Hiring an appraiser can be expensive. It usually runs about $300 - $500, so you will want to work with an experienced real estate agent or mortgage broker with access to home sales data in order to get a more accurate idea of value without spending a fortune.

Important Note on Decreasing Property Values:

If you discover that the homeowners owe more on the property than your ideal purchase price can support, then you will have to negotiate with lenders to get them to accept less than what they are owed. This is called a short sale.

Important Note On Appraisals, Home Inspections & Title Searches:

You must get an appraisal, title inspection and home inspection performed in order to get all of the relevant facts about a property. Now, whether you get a purchased contract signed with contingencies or you pay for these three *before* you get a signed contract, is up to you.

However, I strongly recommend that you have a purchase contract signed with contingencies that state the appraisal, title inspection and home inspection have to meet the buyer's approval because appraisal, title inspection and home inspection could easily cost $1,500 or more.

Step 8: Negotiating With Property Owners

After you have done your research and homework, now it is time for the real work to begin. You must now negotiate with the property owners. One of the important things you must realize is that many homeowners who are in foreclosure are not bad people. However, there are many who try to place the blame on other people for their misfortune. So, now we will take a closer look at the mindset of a distressed homeowner:

- Usually do not want to sell their home.
- Will not negotiate with you if they do not like or trust you.
- Do not want you to show up at their house with an "I Buy Foreclosures" sign on your car.

Okay, so now that you know the mindset of the property owner in foreclosure, here are some basic rules you must also know about negotiating.

1. Only negotiate with the homeowners directly. No middleman.
2. Do not be confrontational. Be cool, calm and collected, no matter what happens.
3. Adopt a trust-but-verify attitude. Whether an accident occurs or the homeowner uses deception, mistakes do happen. Therefore you must verify every piece of information.
4. Be a no-nonsense professional.
5. Be willing to give up small things that do not matter to you if they do not affect the purchase price.

Step 9: Close On The Property

Once you have negotiated a price with the property owner and you have completed the appraisal, home inspection and title search, then it is time to complete the purchase agreements and get them signed.

Now, I know that is a lot and it may seem overwhelming, which is why I say it is not for the first-time homebuyer or someone who is not really a strong negotiator.

Not to be harsh, but I will tell you right up front that if you are not the kind of person who is willing to invest a lot of time, money and energy into buying a foreclosure, then this strategy is definitely NOT for you. However, for the right person, pre-foreclosures can mean HUGE profits. The question is: Are you the right person to do all of the steps I listed above and cross the finish line with the gold?

Pre-Foreclosure Investing Advantages:

- You will often be the first to reach these bargains.
- You will be dealing with the sellers and if there is equity you will not have to negotiate a short sell with the bank.
- The sellers may be more flexible with price because they have a chance to avoid the humiliation of being evicted from their home.

Pre-Foreclosure Investing Disadvantages:

- Requires the buyer to have expertise in several key areas, without the help of a real estate agent to negotiate the terms.
- You have to find the deals, contact the homeowners and negotiate the terms.
- You may have to spend hundreds of dollars before finding one deal.
- High level of rejection.
- Homeowners are emotional and may not even be considering selling.
- You will personally have to negotiate with lenders, collection departments and attorneys.

CHAPTER 5

Strategy #2:
Buying Foreclosures At Auctions

Buying foreclosures at auctions is probably one of the most romanticized forms of investing. However, purchasing a foreclosure at auction is also one of the riskiest forms of investing and requires a lot of real estate expertise.

For example, you are not allowed to inspect the house personally with your own team of professionals prior to purchase. Another example is the fact that you will not receive a refund if you are selected as the bid winner, and are unable to close on the purchase.

Now, we will begin by looking at the steps involved in purchasing foreclosures at auctions:

Step 1: Get Your Mortgage Lined Up

The first step when buying foreclosures at auctions is for you to get pre-approved for a mortgage. Getting pre-approved is even more important when it comes to purchasing at a foreclosure auction. When you are selected as the winning bidder at a foreclosure auction, there is usually no refund given if you cannot get financing.

Step 2: Write Down Your Goals, Needs & Wants For a Foreclosure

Once you have been pre-approved for a mortgage, your next step is to match up your likes, dislikes and goals with what you can actually afford. So, you will need to make a written list of things that you cannot live without or things you can. This is even more important when purchasing a foreclosure at auction, because you have little to no recourse if you win the bid, but change your mind because the home does not meet your needs.

Step 3: Find A Foreclosure Auction

This is one of the most important steps in the process because if you cannot find a bargain that makes you money, then you do not have a deal. Fortunately, locating homeowners who are several months behind on their payments and who are also knocking on the door of foreclosure is not too difficult to find in our current real estate market.

There are several ways to find these types of bargains, so here are my proven methods.

1. Checking the newspapers for upcoming foreclosure sales, known as legal notices. Contact those owners directly and see if they are interested in selling their home.
2. Asking local real estate agents who specialize in foreclosure sales. You can find these agents by checking the home seller's magazines for the distressed seller listings.
3. Subscribe to an online foreclosure list service, which sends you targeted listings matching your needs in your area.

Step 4: Contact the Foreclosing Attorney And Get A Bidders Package.

Contact the attorney or trustee's office that is conducting the foreclosure auction and get the critical information about minimum bid amounts, deposit amount requirements and date and time of auction.

Once you have the bidder's package, you can then go about getting contractors quotes and estimates based on the information provided in the package. Now, one big disadvantage that you will have to navigate when investing in auction foreclosures is the fact that you, your contractors or rehabbers will not get into the house to see the property first hand. The property will be sold as-is with no expectation of negotiating.

Step 5: Hire A Real Estate Attorney

After you have received all of the relevant information about the auction date, location and property, you need to immediately hire an experienced real estate attorney to review all documents that you will be signing and perform a title search. Never assume that the lenders and foreclosing attorney are disclosing all the information that you will need to bid effectively.

Order a complete title search from a local attorney on the property so you know all existing liens and stakeholders for the property. Title searches can cost you anywhere from $200 - $500.

Step 6: Determine the home value

Now, in order for you to know that you are getting a bargain at an auction, you must get an appraisal performed on the home. However, because it is an auction purchase you will have an appraisal ordered by the courts, but you will not be allowed to have your appraiser inside the house.

So, you can get an estimated range of the market value of the property by having a drive-by appraisal performed, or having a real estate agent perform a comparative market analysis (CMA).

Hiring an appraiser can be expensive. It usually runs about $300 - $500, so you will want to work with an experienced real estate agent or mortgage broker with access to home sales data in order to get a more accurate idea of value without spending a fortune.

Important Note On Appraisals, Home Inspections & Title Searches:

When you are purchasing at an auction you will not have a chance to get an appraisal, title inspection and home inspection performed. This is the primary reason that there is more risk involved in buying at auctions. However, you must still get these inspections performed after you have won the bid on the house. These inspections give you vital information, which you need to know as the new owner.

Step 7: Auction Day

On the day of the foreclosure auction there are several things you must do in order to bid effectively. They are:

- Call the attorney or trustee's office and verify that the auction is still happening. Many times homeowners will file bankruptcy or get an extension prior to the auction.

- Review the deposit amount required, location and time of the auction.

- Make sure to have a certified bank check for the deposit.

- Know the value of the property you are bidding on.

- Establish your highest price that you will be able to bid up to by reviewing all repairs you will be making, your maximum mortgage amount and the overall cost of owning the home.

Step 8: Attend The Auction & Bid

When you arrive at the auction find the person in charge of the auction and ask for the paperwork that spells out how the auction will be conducted. After you review the rules, be prepared to start bidding.

The bidding might be like a traditional auction or it might be a silent auction, which means you write down your offer on a piece of paper and the highest bidder wins.

Step 9: Winner or Loser?

Upon winning the bid, your deposit is applied towards the purchase price and you will most likely have thirty days to ninety days to close on the property. If you lose the bid, then you simply regroup and move on to the next potential property that fits your investing criteria.

The Advantages Of Buying Foreclosures At Auctions:

- There are more properties going to auction these days, so there is more opportunity.
- You will not have to negotiate a short sell with the bank.
- If there are few bidders, you may be able to get an even better deal than you would if you were negotiating directly with the bank.
- You will usually know the closing date well in advance so you can be prepared.
- Most times you will also get a due diligence packet of all the information about the property.

The Disadvantages Of Buying Foreclosures At Auctions:

- Most times, you do not have the benefit of walking through the house and previewing it.
- You cannot have the home inspected prior to purchasing the home.
- You may be forced to overpay by the nature of the bidding process.
- Usually by the time of the auction the house has been vacant and not taken care of for months at a time.
- You may possibly have to evict the current homeowner turned squatters. It could get very ugly and you may accumulate thousands of dollars in extra fees before you even move in.

CHAPTER 6

Strategy #3:
Buying Bank-Owned Properties
After The Auction

Over my years of helping hundreds of investors purchase their first property I have come to the conclusion that buying bank-owned or REO (Real Estate Owned) is one of the safest, yet profitable ways to purchase foreclosures. The benefits are numerous, but here are a couple of my top favorites:

- The bank usually does some repairs to get the home into saleable condition.
- You can have home inspections and appraisals performed on the property, unlike when you are buying at a foreclosure auction.
- You get to walk through the house before you buy it. Unlike when you purchase at the auction.
- You do not have to evict the current occupants.
- You can possibly get a bargain price on a home that is in move-in condition.

Now, to be perfectly honest with you, bank-owned properties are technically not properties that are currently in foreclosure. Bank-owned properties are homes that the owners were foreclosed upon and the banks could not or would not sell them at auction. The previous owners have already been evicted, so the hard part has been done already.

So, let's get started on the eight steps you will need to take in order to purchase a bank-owned property or REO property.

Step 1: Get Pre-Approved For A Mortgage

Not to sound like a broken record, but just like with any of the other foreclosure investing strategies, you need to get pre-approved first. Enough said about that, I hope.

Step 2: Write Down Your Goals, Needs & Wants For a Foreclosure Bargain

Once again, just like with the other foreclosure investing strategies, you need to know exactly what you are looking for in a home before you start presenting offers or bidding on properties. Do this by writing and listing your needs, wants and goals, and carry them with you everywhere in case you discover one that needs to be added or removed.

Step 3: Find a Real Estate Agent With Expertise In Bank-Owned & REO Homes

When you purchase a bank-owned property, you must work with a real estate agent who is very experienced in negotiating with banks. There is a huge difference between negotiating with another seller's agent and negotiating with a bank. In fact, with rare exception, you should never purchase a bank-owned property without going through a real estate agent.

The number one method for finding a quality real estate agent is to ask your friends, family and co-workers for a recommendation of a real estate agent that they have used in the past. Then you will want to go online to the National Association of Exclusive Buyers Agents, at www.naeba.org to cross-reference their name to see if they specialize as buyers' agents only. Just keep in mind that their referred agent may or may not specialize in finding bank-owned bargains. It is an investing niche that requires substantial expertise, and not every agent masters this area.

The second way to find an agent is to look online. This is an easy way to do it. You can instantly find out which agents are really moving and shaking when it comes to having bank-owned properties for sale. However, keep in mind that these agents represent the banks, so you will want to enter in search terms like "shoreline condo buyer's agent" to get more specific search results when looking online.

It is also worth your time to visit realtor.com or activerain.com and use the search function on their website to find local agents who specialize in helping buyers find bank-owned bargains.

However, one of the most underrated strategies I have seen is to search through the home browser magazines that come out every week. You can browse through and see the agents for whatever area you want to live in, and you will find agents who specialize in bank-owned properties.

Step 4: Visit The Top Homes That Meet Your Criteria And Make An Offer.

After your real estate agent has selected several homes that meet your criteria, then it is time for you to walk through each one and begin to narrow down your options until you find one that you like.

Once you find a suitable home, then submit your offer bid. I think it is worth noting that your negotiating strategy when dealing with a bank is different than when negotiating with a homeowner. Banks tend to take up to thirty days to respond, so if you are only submitting low-ball offers, then expect them to take thirty to sixty days to tell you no. Your strategy has to focus on finding a suitable middle ground that allows both you and the bank to make a profit.

Step 5: Once Your Offer Is Accepted, Then Get Appraisal And Home Inspection Completed.

Once your offer is accepted it is time to get an appraisal, home inspection and title search completed. Your real estate agent and loan officer will work together to make sure these steps are completed, but just like when you buy at a auction or pre-foreclosure, you will have to spend the money out of pocket.

Step 6: Close On The Property And Move In.
When the appraisal, home inspection and title search are completed and the results are normal or satisfactory, then your mortgage lender will set up a time to close on the property.

Buying Bank-Owned Properties Summary

Buying a bank-owned home or REO is just like buying a regular home on the market. That is the reason why I recommend it to most people who want to get into foreclosure investing, but do not want to risk losing the shirt off their back.

See, when you buy bank-owned properties, you have a chance to get your own appraisal, home inspection and title search completed and still have the option to withdraw your offer, if the results you find do not meet your liking. This is very different from buying at a foreclosure auction where you are forced to close in thirty days and leave a fifteen to thirty thousand dollar deposit, just to bid! You also do not have to deal with emotional homeowners who are looking for every other option on the planet that does not include selling their home to you, like when you are investing in pre-foreclosures.

The Advantages of Buying Bank-Owned Homes:

- The bank usually does some repairs to get the home into saleable condition.
- You can have home inspections and appraisals performed on the property, unlike when you are buying at a foreclosure auction.
- You get to walk through the house before you buy it, unlike when you purchase at the auction.
- You do not have to evict the current occupants.
- You can possibly get a bargain price on a home that is in move-in condition.

The Disadvantages of Buying Bank-Owned Homes:

- You may not get the deep, deep discounts like you could possibly get at a foreclosure auction or buying a pre-foreclosure.
- Banks negotiate at their own pace and with their own terms. Many times this can take months to wrap up.

CHAPTER 7

Creating Your Foreclosure "Dream Team": Loan Officer/Mortgage Broker

One of the most important skills that many other foreclosure-investing books skim over quickly or neglect completely is the team building and people managing component of investing in foreclosures. See, no matter which foreclosure investing strategy you choose, you will be required to use at least four of the following six real estate professionals, and most likely all six.

- Loan Officer/Mortgage Broker
- Real Estate Agent
- Real Estate Attorney
- Appraiser
- Home Inspector
- Home Improvement Contractor

There are simply too many pitfalls and money pits to fall into when investing in foreclosures to go at it alone. In fact, the difference between not using a qualified and experienced real estate professional can literally mean tens of thousands of dollars in additional costs, expensive lawsuits and hundreds of lost hours of peace of mind. In this chapter, I not only reveal how you can find the best professionals in your area, but also give you the right questions to ask and tips to use when negotiating price and terms for their services. After all, you want to make sure you have the best and brightest professionals on your foreclosure-investing team.

Team Member #1: Loan Officer/Mortgage Broker

Unless you are already very wealthy, you will need to finance your foreclosure purchase. Therefore, you will need to hire a loan officer or mortgage broker to arrange the financing for you. A good loan officer is worth his weight in gold. There will be times when a deal can seem to fall apart because of low appraisal values or problems uncovered during the inspection or contract negotiations. However, if you have an experienced loan officer, he will have dealt with this before and will have years of experience to draw from to get everybody back on board.

It may come as a surprise to you, but not all mortgage lenders are created equal. As a matter of fact, the majority of mortgage lenders do not have access or knowledge of the best mortgage programs. However, it is not entirely their fault. They just happen to work for banks or companies that only allow them to offer homebuyers a few simple choices. Unfortunately, that means that you, the bargain hunter, may miss out on some of the juiciest programs. So, try to choose a mortgage broker when buying a foreclosure, as they usually have access to the best programs.

There are two main types of mortgage providers who can provide you with a mortgage.

- **Direct Lender/Mortgage Bank** – These are banks, credit unions or any other type of financial institution that loans you their own money. They benefit directly from your mortgage payments each month as you pay off your interest. They will often "sell" your mortgage for an upfront fee to another investor who views the interest as a return. Direct lenders usually charge a little less for providing your mortgage, but only have access to their mortgage programs. They also tend to not have a wide variety of down payment assistance and mortgage programs.

- **Mortgage Broker** – These are independently authorized mortgage companies which do not lend their own money, but act as middleman to dozens of mortgage programs offered by many banks all over the nation. Mortgage brokers tend to charge slightly higher fees, but have unlimited access to mortgage programs and down payment assistance programs, which can add up to tens of thousands of dollars in savings over the life of your loan. Mortgage brokers are especially useful when you buy a foreclosure because they have specialized expertise.

After many years of counseling homebuyers after they have come to me after working with other mortgage professionals, I am convinced there is only one smart way to find a mortgage professional.

1. Ask for a referral from a friend, family member or co-worker that has worked with a specific mortgage professional.
   Special Note: If a friend refers you to a bank, then ask them for a specific contact person to ask for. If they do not remember specifically, then when you call or visit, politely ask for the most experienced specialist that they have on staff.

2. If you cannot get a referral, then select one local bank that you currently bank with and one local mortgage brokerage that specialize in the type of property you are buying.

However, what you should **NOT** do is:

- **Call around for rate quotes** - There are some loan officers who will give you a low-ball rate, which they cannot possibly follow through on. This is just a deceptive ploy to get your business.

- **Compare annual percentage rates** - Many lenders use several different factors to come up with APR. Very rarely do two banks use the same formula.

- **Compare ads** - The ads are to get you into the office to sign up. Mortgage companies put the most attractive information that applies for less than 1% of the population to bait and switch you.

My reasoning for primarily using this strategy of getting a referral and not "shopping around" is simple. There is no way you should be talking to a mystery voice on the phone during the most exciting yet stressful financial decision of your life. You need someone you can see face to face when things get rough. Someone you can locate easily whenever you have a question. More importantly, you need someone you can trust.

Questions To Ask A Loan Officer or Mortgage Broker

The next step, once you find a good mortgage professional, is to interview him or her to see if this will be a good fit for you. Here are some of the questions you should ask:

- Are you a mortgage broker, banker or direct lender?
- Are you licensed by the state, and have any complaints ever been filed against you?
- Have you ever worked with foreclosure investors before?
- Do you have real estate agents, inspectors or home improvement contractors contacts, just in case I need them?
- Is the interest rate you will quote me fixed or adjustable?
- Do you lock in the interest rate, and if so, for how long?
- What is your fee for doing the mortgage?
- What additional fees will be added to the mortgage besides yours?
- Will my loan be sold?
- Will I have a prepayment penalty?
- If I pay for the appraisal, will you immediately give me a copy of it when you receive it?
- If I pay for the credit report, will you immediately give me a copy of it?
- Who do I contact to get a copy of the closing documents 24 hours before closing?
- How long will it take to get me an approval?
- Can you send me a good faith estimate showing all fees?

Once the loan officer has answered all of the questions above, then you will need to begin answering their questions in order to get your mortgage pre-approval.

7 Reasons Why You Should Work With Your Local Mortgage Professional Or Risk Disaster

1. You can meet face-to-face to interview your local mortgage professional.

2. You can talk to the local mortgage professional face to face if there is a problem.

3. Your local mortgage professional can attend the closing and help with any errors that show up last minute.

4. Your local mortgage professional will be familiar with local real estate market trends.

5. Your local mortgage professional will have relationships with the attorney and title company actually performing your closing.

6. Your local mortgage professional will know the standard local fees that are charged.

7. Your local mortgage professional is more likely to have a visible and easily reachable team to help out during the process.

CHAPTER 8

Creating Your Foreclosure "Dream Team": Real Estate Agent

Many of the foreclosure investing books and programs that I have read over the years do not mention anything about the value of using a real estate agent. Most of the get-rich quick foreclosure investing gurus tell you that you can do it all by yourself, without the help of a real estate agent. However, that could not be further from the truth. In fact, the only time that you should purchase a foreclosure without a real estate agent is when you are buying at auction.

Here is a breakdown of when to use a real estate agent.

Investing Strategy	Agent Required
Pre-foreclosure Investing	Yes
Buying At Auction	No
Bank-Owned & REO	Yes

A real estate agent is a professional who has a state authorized license to help you buy (or sell) your home. They act as your agent to negotiate prices with the seller so that a transaction can be finalized, allowing you to buy your new home.

A good real estate agent is also worth their weight in gold and helps you:
- Hone in on your true needs and wants
- Find a home you like which meets your goals
- Get the background information on the property
- Put together an offer price to give to seller

- Negotiate with the sellers
- Find other real estate professionals to help you
- Be your go-to person for the whole purchase transaction
- Put together the purchase and sales contract

Types of Real Estate Agents

There are three different levels of experience, knowledge and training when it comes to real estate agents. The differences are very important because you can reasonably expect a certain level of knowledge and expertise when working with each type of real estate agent.:

> **Real Estate Agent** – A professional who has completed several months of training and classroom education and been authorized by the state. This is the most basic level of real estate agents.

> **Realtors®** - These are real estate agents or brokers who are members of the National Association of Realtors®. Their membership allows them to use a special designation, however they are held to a much higher standard than the average real estate agent. A Realtor® will have more education and certifications as well. You will want to find an Accredited Buyer Representative (ABR) or Accredit Buyer Representative Manager (ABRM). This means they specialize in representing buyers. Your goal should always be to work with Realtors® because they usually have the highest level of experience and education.

> **Real Estate Brokers** – Brokers have more education and knowledge than a basic real estate agent. Brokers usually own the agency and also manage a team of agents. Acts like a business owner in many regards.

Finding Your Own Buyer's Agent

Finding a good real estate agent who is knowledgeable, experienced and trustworthy should be your number one priority. However, you must be sure the real estate agent's expertise matches up as closely as possible with requirements you created when you first started the foreclosure buying process. Once that is done you must consider the following variables with every real estate agent you may be considering:

- **Location** – Don't hire a real estate agent who only works in a certain county and you live three counties over. A real estate agent who knows the neighborhood is even more important when you are buying foreclosure properties.
- **Style** – There are some real estate agents who only specialize in hotels and occasionally take on a buyer or two for residential property. You should avoid them at all costs unless you are looking for a hotel.
- **Construction** – Many homebuyers would love to purchase newly constructed homes, but did you know that these homes have a whole different set of issues, and unless real estate agent specializes in these he or she will not have a clue.
- **Size** – Sounds obvious, but over the years I have seen many people let real estate agents convince them to buy homes that were too big and too small...all because they loved how the house looked.
- **Age** – The newer the home the more likely that it will have the bells and whistles you might like. The older the home the more you might have to update once you move in. An experienced real estate agent will know this.
- **Functionality** – An experienced agent will ask you questions about your lifestyle to find those little "extras" that make you glad you bought your home.
- **Land** – Unbelievable as it might sound there are some of us who actually *need* a 96-acre lake to bass fish every weekend. However, if that is your dream home and your real estate agent specializes in land-locked condos, you might be in for a bit of a disappointment.

Recommended Methods To Find A Real Estate Agent

The number one method for finding a quality real estate agent is to ask your friends, family and co-workers for a recommendation. Then you will want to go online to the National Association of Exclusive Buyers Agents, at www.naeba.org to cross-reference their name to see if they specialize as buyers' agents only. You will learn why that is so important a little later on, but for the next five minutes just trust me.

The second way to find an agent is to look online. This is an easy way to do it. You can instantly find out which agents are really moving and shaking when it comes to having houses for sale. However, keep in mind that these agents represent the sellers, so you will want to enter in search terms like "shoreline condo buyer's agent" to get more specific search results when looking online.

It is also worth your time to visit realtor.com or activerain.com. However one of the most underrated strategies I have seen is to actually enter the search term "exclusive buyer brokerage, no listings" for whatever area you want to live in and you will find agents who specialize in working with buyers just like you.

The Worst Way To Find A Good Real Estate Agent

Attending open houses in order to find an agent is like rolling the dice. The agent who is doing the open house may or may not be the listing agent, BUT they absolutely know the listing agent and thus is more likely to be torn between negotiating the best price for you and helping out their buddy. This is not guaranteed to happen, but in my experience is just more likely to happen. However, with that being said, visiting open houses is a good opportunity to find out about the house and what comparable houses are selling for.

CHAPTER 9

Creating Your Foreclosure "Dream Team": Real Estate Attorney

As a foreclosure buyer, you will have plenty of legitimate things to worry about, so you will need to take as much off your plate as reasonably possible. In this section I am going to review the huge benefits of hiring your own personal attorney when investing in foreclosures.

However, I must give you a word of caution before jumping right in. There are many people (including real estate professionals) who will tell you that you do not need your own attorney to buy your foreclosure. When someone tells you that, turn right around and ask them, "Are you willing to study for six months to take an all-day grueling test, then spend upwards of two hundred thousand dollars to attend college for six to eight years to represent me in court for two or three years in case my mortgage paperwork has an honest mistake?" If they say yes, then tell them when you are in the market to buy a house in ten years you will allow them to represent you then, but as for now you will prefer to go with an established real estate attorney. If they say no, then tell them you will feel more comfortable with someone who will!

Those people giving you that advice are also the same people who believe a closing agent or real estate attorney provided by the seller or lender actually works for you, the buyer, to protect you during the foreclosure buying process. Well, let me the first to tell you that it is not true. The attorney who performs the closing for the lender or seller is there to protect the lender or seller, not you.

Everyone has an opinion about whether or not you need your own attorney when buying a home, but who will actually volunteer to be your legal representation when you are in dire straits? Now, here is the reality of risk that is associated every time anyone decides to buy a home:

- It is the biggest financial decision of your life, so you will be nervous. When most people are nervous, they forget even the simplest of things.
- You could lose your deposit because of a technicality in the wording of the contract.
- One little incorrect phrasing of a contingency could hold you legally obligated to buy a home you no longer want.
- There are some crooks in the real estate professional that will rob you blind.
- You will be legally held responsible for your home for the next thirty plus years.
- Your housing payment will consume a majority of one, if not two, of your monthly paychecks.
- You are legally responsible if someone falls in your house, yard and possibly sidewalk in front of your house.

Real estate lawyers are experienced in all of the laws and regulations that are involved in the buying and selling of a home and other property. If you are like most people, then you also do not understand the complex language of the many contracts that you will be required to sign, from offering to closing, and a lawyer is the best way to make sure you are protected. They can explain all the legal terms so that you understand them. They can also advise you on whether or not the deal you are looking at is the right one for you and your needs. Basically, a real estate lawyer will protect you from being tricked, robbed, or landing in financial ruin.

It never seems to fail that foreclosure buyers run into one or two problems that will require the expertise of an attorney. It may not happen during the first property purchase or the second, but Murphy's Law tends to work in bizarre ways. Instead of tempting fate and letting a problem sneak in unannounced, reduce your chances of making a costly mistake by using a reliable and experienced real estate attorney

Examples of Real-Life Situations That Happen

There is nothing wrong with admitting that you need help when it comes to legal contracts. Most people do not understand what they are reading unless they already work in some form of legal profession and deal with contracts on a daily basis. It is better to retain a lawyer than take the chance of something going wrong that you cannot easily fix, or that will leave you in financial ruin. Additionally, difficult sellers with unusual or unreasonable requests can be shot down when you have a lawyer with you who has the gall to say no when a real estate agent does not. When things get really strange, a lawyer in your corner will always make sure you are protected.

We will take a look at a few examples of where an attorney can definitely be a life – and financial – saver:

- You are at the closing of your home and you are presented with a different type of deed than what you and your agent originally agreed upon. If you have retained a lawyer, you would simply postpone the closing until the lawyer could look over the deed and then give you an acceptable warranty deed in place of the one that was presented to you by the seller.
- The seller of the home is procrastinating in a way that seems like they are trying to kill the sale *after* you have already signed the purchase and sale contract. The seller could be trying to accept an offer higher than the one they agreed to from you. In this case, the lawyer will step in and let the seller know that you have legal rights and that they will file a 'lis pendens.' This questions the property's ownership and could very well prove that the seller was trying to do something very underhanded.
- Your potential bargain home has a title issue that relates to the back taxes owed to the IRS by the previous owner. A capable real estate lawyer will be able to advise you on your rights and help you clear up the problem with the IRS before you close on the house. The IRS problems are the seller's problems that they are trying to dump on you. Your lawyer could propose a compromise prior to the final closing that must be met or the deal is off until the IRS issue is fixed. If

you sign off on the home before the IRS issues are resolved, you may become liable for them once you sign the papers.

- When buying a pre-foreclosure, if the seller offers to do work on the home to finish something they started or to repair a problem that is outstanding, get it in writing and have the lawyer look over it to make sure everything is legal.
- Days before you close on your home your lawyer and real estate agent discover that the seller sold the house to someone else but did not file the paperwork showing the sale yet. Your lawyer could go in and file a copy of your sales contract with the court, beating out the other claimant and clouding the title for anyone else the seller may try to sell the home to.

The above situation has been prevented in many cases by the passing of a law that allows real estate lawyers to file a contract of affidavit with the courts stating that there is a sale pending on the home and that it will be closed on in a set amount of time. This helps the courts keep a track of what is going on in the real estate market and keeps double filings on one property from happening.

As you can see, having a real estate lawyer in your corner is really a good idea, especially when investing in foreclosures. They know and understand all of the legal wrangling that may need to take place in order to get property bought and sold without any surprises for both parties involved. As I mentioned earlier, a lawyer is not a requirement, but definitely an asset in your corner.

The Many Hats of A Real Estate Attorney

A real estate attorney performs a variety of functions from the time they are put on retainer to the time the final paperwork is signed and you as the buyer take possession of the residence. Real estate lawyers handle contract reviews, mortgage paperwork, and researching liens and more. We will take a look at some of these functions and how they affect you in the purchasing process.

- **Real estate lawyers will review your contract and mortgage paperwork** - The wording of a real estate contract can be very hard to understand. The average person may not be able to comprehend all of the legal terminology, and the services of a real estate lawyer can help you. You never want to sign any form of legal binding document without understanding what the terms and conditions really mean.

  In fact, by the time you arrive at your mortgage closing, your money has most likely already been transferred from the lender who is providing your mortgage to the seller's mortgage company hours before you ever sign the final paperwork. This is something the average investor and seller are not aware of. When you have a real estate lawyer on retainer, they will review your mortgage paperwork to make sure that there are no hidden issues that you need to be aware of before signing paperwork and taking possession of your new home. Real estate lawyers are there to protect you and your assets.

- **Real estate lawyers will look for and fix any outstanding property liens before you close** - When you prepare to purchase a home, there could be a hidden issue lurking in the background that will come to light during the selling and buying process. A real estate lawyer's job is to search the public records for any issues that may be outstanding. These ownership issues could be unpaid back taxes that are owed to the government, money that is owed for repairs, or anything that is less than legal in the eyes of the law – in other words, possible shady dealings the current homeowner has been engaged in to sell the home. While these are just a few of the issues that could surface during a title search, there could be more that could be even more devastating to you and your finances.

  If your real estate lawyer finds any issues, they will alert you. Searching the public records usually only takes a day or two, thanks to the connections the lawyer already has established with the local courthouses and title search companies. A title search is the most important aspect of buying a home because of the ramifications an undiscovered issue can cause. When an issue is found and everyone is notified, the lawyer will work with you and your real estate agent to develop possible options to solve the issue. They could suggest a price reduction so the issue can be satisfied and summarily dismissed upon taking possession of the home. They will also suggest ways the seller can rectify the problem efficiently and easily without having to run around like a chicken with its head cut off. Plus, the lawyer will be able to recommend solutions that meet the requirements of your new lender. Once a legal solution is put into place, the sale can go forward without a hitch.

- **A real estate lawyer can handle all of the filing issues related to your purchase -** When you purchase a home, the deed passes to you from the seller. This deed needs to be filed with the county and state in which you live. Sometimes the property you purchase is zoned in a way that you will not be able to perform certain types of construction on it. A real estate lawyer will be able to take care of getting the property deed filed quickly and they will also be able to help you understand what the state stipulations surrounding your property are so that you can move on with the sale, armed with foreknowledge.

Selecting Your Real Estate Attorney

The guidelines for selecting a real estate attorney use the same formula for selecting each of your real estate professionals.

1. Select three local law firms to talk with.
2. One of the above should be a referral from a friend, family member or co-worker that has previously worked with the real estate attorney professional.
3. Ask for a specific person to work with, then meet with them to discuss your goals and see if there is a good fit.

I realize my formula is simple, but do not minimize the effectiveness of its simplicity. As I have said before, you can't put your trust in the hands of the lender's or seller's attorney to protect you during the most exciting yet stressful financial decision of your life. You need someone in your corner in case things get rough. Someone you know has your back whenever you have a question. More importantly, you need someone you can trust.

Things To Remember When Interviewing A Real Estate Attorney

The first thing you need to be aware of is that this meeting should be conducted professionally. It is a business meeting and your lawyer will be presenting him or herself with the utmost decorum. You may think that this seems a bit extreme, but it is not. Dress nicely, be on time, be cordial and polite, and above all else, be confident in yourself, your lawyer and the purchase you are about to make. Impress your lawyer and they will impress you with their knowledge and skill. Here are some specific things to do when you first meet with your lawyer.

- **Get to know your lawyer and give them the chance to get to know you.** Tell them why you are looking for a home at this particular junction in your life and why you feel you need their services. As you converse, gauge the lawyer's level of interest in taking you on as a client. This first meeting will give each of you a feel for the other before making a business agreement that should be beneficial.
- **Listen to what your attorney has to say and do not explain everything in the beginning.** Just let him know that you want to invest in foreclosures and want to protect yourself while making a profit. Remember, most likely the real estate attorney has helped numerous clients that have been in the same position as you have and they understand your needs.
- **If at all possible, bring all of the documentation you have collected on the purchase with you and present it to your lawyer when asked.** By providing them with this paperwork

now, you save valuable time and money running back and forth with the bits and pieces of the process.

- **Once you find a lawyer you will work with, do not be afraid to tell your lawyer everything – good and bad –** in order to make sure they are equipped with all of the information they need ahead of time. There is nothing worse than having your lawyer shocked over a piece of information that should've been revealed from the onset. Anything you say to the lawyer is confidential and will remain that way, even if you do not hire the lawyer and go with someone else.

- **Let your lawyer worry about the issues that you have no control over.** They will be able to tell you if the issues are to your benefit. This is why you have hired them. They understand the legal ramifications of many issues and they will be able to offer you possible solutions. They will help you make sure your ultimate goals are met.

- **If you feel that a lawyer is not a good fit for you, you have the right to decline their services.** The same goes for the lawyer. If the lawyer is willing to represent you, they will be confident that everything will run smoothly. Feel free to ask them questions, including whether or not they are comfortable representing you during this transaction. Find out if the lawyer will be working on your sale exclusively, or if others will be assisting, and if you can meet them.

- **Ask the lawyer what their rates and fees are if you feel that the lawyer is the right one to represent you.**

- **It is okay to tell the lawyer that you want to consider their offer of representations before you sign a contract with them if you have other lawyers to speak with.** If you do decide to sign with the lawyer, have them explain their contract to you and define exactly what services they will be providing and how much they will cost. When you understand how the lawyer will work, sign the contract. Have the retainer payment on hand and request a payment schedule before leaving the office.

- **Make sure you understand when your real estate lawyer will start working on your case and when they think they will have something to report.** Let them know that you will be available to help them if required. Ask that they remain in contact even if there is nothing new going on.

Under the watchful eye of your real estate attorney, the entire transactions should move as smoothly as possible. When you are ready to close on your home, make sure you have your current photo identification with you and any closing fees in the form of certified funds. If your lawyer recommends anything else, make sure you have the documentation at the closing, just in case anything needs to be modified or added by your lawyer during the closing.

Sometimes special circumstances arise and you may need to have someone else sign your papers on your behalf. As soon as you know you will not be able to make it to the closing, contact your attorney and inform them. They will confirm with your lending institution what you will need to do to pass power of attorney to another individual – such as your spouse – or to your lawyer, so that they can sign the papers on your behalf. Also, if you are the sole name on the mortgage and are married, in most states your spouse does not have to sign the mortgage papers or even be present at the closing.

A real estate lawyer is a good investment all around, as they can handle any and all issues that arise during the buying and selling of a home. They will ensure that all of the paperwork is legal and correct and that everything that needs to be filed is done so with the proper authorities and in a timely manner. They are well worth the investment of the retainer fee, especially if something unexpected crops up. With an attorney at your side, your investment is protected.

What Exactly Does A Real Estate Attorney/Closing Agent Do?

Real Estate Attorney does...	However, you still have to do the following...
- Reviews the title report from seller's attorney and secures you title insurance. - Tallies up the daily costs and makes adjustments to insurance, taxes and mortgage interest. - Coordinates payment for taxes and recording fees. - Completes the transfer and recording of deed. - Reviews, collects and makes sure all the necessary paperwork is there for your financing and proper disclosures. - Oversees the payment transfer to seller from your lender.	- Read every single page and document you sign. - Make sure you have a clear understanding on what you are signing off on. - Review and understand the preliminary title report and in order to understand the solutions to overcome any issues that arise. - Ask questions when you do not understand something. - Fork over the cash for the closing costs per your agreement in the purchase and sales contract. - Work together cooperatively with your appraiser, home inspector, mortgage broker and real estate agent.

CHAPTER 10

Creating Your Foreclosure "Dream Team": Appraisers

Believe it or not, there was a time when folks just drove by a house, looked at the outside and then scanned through a database of what houses sold recently to determine the value of a home. However, things have changed. The new rules state that every type of mortgage in this new real estate market requires an appraisal. The fact of the matter is, you will not get approved for a home mortgage without it.

If you are buying a foreclosure as an investment, the appraisal value is very important to you. A good appraisal could mean the difference between pocketing tens of thousands of dollars or walking away with next to nothing. If you are buying a foreclosure as your primary residence, then you should be a little more willing to allow a lower value to be okay, because you plan on living there for a longer period of time, which allows the value to appreciate.

An appraisal is an estimate of the home value you are considering purchasing. The appraisal value is an opinion of value by a licensed appraiser who walks around the inside and outside of the home, inspects and verifies the square footage, overall condition of the home and makes sure everything looks like it is in working condition, or at least could be at some point in the near future. An appraiser also takes into consideration what other similar homes have sold for in recent months when calculating the value.

After doing the visual inspection and the research on the history of the home, the appraiser then takes a couple of days to put together a detailed and comprehensive report of his findings and will compare the appraised home to the sale prices of similar types of houses in the neighborhood. All of the work that the appraiser is doing comes down to one thing: determining the value of the home that is being appraised, called the subject property.

By the way, there is no limit to the amount of comparisons that can be made to other homes in order to really get the best snapshot of the home value. The most popular home comparisons are square footage, inside and outside condition of the home, amenities such as marble floors or granite counter tops, and just the basic overall condition.

It is also important to note that based on what the appraiser finds in his visual inspection and research, a home's value can be increased or decreased because of what other properties are selling for in the same area. However, as a general rule of thumb, a single family home with 3 bedrooms and two bathrooms will, in most cases, appraise for a slightly higher value than a home within the same neighborhood with the same general interior and exterior and only 2 bedrooms and one bathroom. Another example would be if a home has a front and backyard that looks like a jungle; it will generally appraise for a lower value than the same house next door, simply because of the lack of landscaping.

What is Market Value?

The easiest way to think of market value is to view it as the price the home could be sold for if the seller's had to sell the home in the next sixty to ninety days. Additionally, it also means that:

- Both the buyer and seller are trying to get the best price possible.
- The buyer and seller have a fair amount of knowledge about the home.
- There is an easily explainable and reasonable time frame that the house has been on the market.
- The seller is being paid in good ole' fashion American dollars.
- There are no creative or special under the table money arrangements reflected in the price.

Come on down! The Price Is NOT Right!

In theory, if a home seller hires an appraiser to come up with a value for their home and the buyer hires a separate appraiser to come up with a value, both should be within a few thousand of each other. Now that is theory. In real life I have seen thirty, forty and even fifty thousand dollar swings in value from one appraisal to the next...on the same house! So be prepared to have to fight for the value of the home if your appraiser comes up with a value which is substantially less than the seller's think the house is worth.

Appraisals Give You Additional Protection

The main reason you want a licensed and experienced appraiser is to keep everybody inside the boxing ring and fighting fair. This includes the lender who does not want to loan out more money than a home could be sold for in a fair market. This also includes the buyer like YOU who does not want to get raked over the coals by some greedy seller, bank or auctioneer. The appraisal is like the last line of defense for you as a buyer if your real estate agent is not successful in pulling in the reins on a home that is selling for too much.

Your appraisal must be done by a licensed appraiser who can readily produce proof of having a state issued license to determine home values. So your friend who has bought and sold a lot of houses does not qualify, unless he or she has an appraisals license. The other side of the coin is the appraiser has to be approved to do appraisals for the specific lender that is providing your mortgage.

Additionally, you will not be at the house when the appraiser does his inspection and walk through. Chances are that you will know the day, but not the exact time the appraiser will be at the seller's home.

The Source of Comparable Home Information

The appraiser gathers the property value information from several sources such as tax records located at the court house in the town the home is located, the multiple listing services (MLS) and flood zone data from the Federal Emergency Management Association (FEMA). This is where the exact details about the home come into play such as the size, condition, location and every possible specific piece of data that you could imagine.

There is also an X-factor involved in the appraisal process that many foreclosure investors are unaware of. It is the appraiser's past experience from the value of the subject property or other homes in the neighborhood.

How Do You Hire An Appraiser

Your mortgage lender will usually coordinate the hiring of an appraiser for your prospective home. Unless you only want to know the value to satisfy your curiosity, there is very few times that a foreclosure investor will seek out and hire an appraiser. The reason why homebuyers do not hire appraisers directly is because the mortgage lender determines if the appraiser is approved to perform the appraisal. Would you want to spend $400 for an appraisal only to learn that your mortgage lender will not accept the appraisal?

Even though you will not normally be required to be involved with hiring your appraiser, you will still want to be involved in this step of the process. It is a good idea to meet your appraiser if it is possible, because after all, you are the one paying them.

The Final Authority On Home Value

When you were calculating your offer price, your real estate agent most likely talked to you about "comparable properties" to determine the value of the home. However, when it comes to figuring out a home value that a lender will approve, it is a totally different ballgame. As crazy as it may sound, the reality is that those comparable properties will usually be very different from the home value that a lender's appraiser will calculate. Be prepared for the numbers to change when it comes to the lender's appraisal.

You Pay For The Appraisal…But Who is The Boss?

This one is a hot issue for foreclosure investors as well as homeowners looking to refinance. The technical answer is that lenders employ the appraisers to give them an idea of the value of the home involved in the transaction. The real life answer is appraisers work for you. After all, you are the one cutting the check to them. The cause for problems is the fact that appraisers always tell you to call your mortgage lender when you request a copy of the appraisal.

Trust me when I tell you that this can become a big hairy tarantula if you ever wanted to switch lenders in the middle of a purchase transaction, because the lender would require that you pay for another appraisal.

The True Owner of "Your" Appraisal

In the majority of cases, the lender orders the appraisal and the homebuyer pays for the appraisal. What this means is lenders hold the end of the leash when it comes to how the appraisal is used and who gets a copy of it. As a homebuyer you have the right to receive a copy of the appraisal, but the lenders control what you can do with it.

The only two times this rule is different is when you are a home owner and you hire a real estate appraiser without a lender being involved. Secondly, if you hire an appraiser without going through a lender, the lender will not accept this appraisal as certified value. Therefore, you will have to pay for another appraisal anyway. Generally speaking, if the appraiser does not tell you that you cannot use the appraisal for a specific purpose, then it is up to you to decide what you will do with the appraisal.

Cost of The Appraisal

The buyers always pay for the appraisal when the appraisal is performed. The appraisal fee usually can cost somewhere between four hundred dollars or more for a single family home. However, there are cases in which an appraisal could cost thousands of dollars. For example, if you are planning on purchasing a fifteen hundred square foot raised ranch, then you might normally expect to pay between four and six hundred dollars. However, if that fifteen hundred square foot raised ranch sits on fifty acres of land, which the lender also wants appraised, then be prepared to open up your checkbook a little wider.

What To Do When Your Appraisal Value Comes Back Lower Than Your Purchase Price

If you find yourself in the situation where the appraised value of a home is lower than what the seller is asking or is lower than the value the lender is willing to lend on, then thank your luck stars and renegotiate your purchase price or move on.

With that being said, appraisals are opinions of value and as opinions go, they can be changed. However, you must use common sense when thinking about the flexibility of your appraiser. If it is a couple of thousand dollars it may be no big deal, but if it is ten to twenty thousand then you probably are on the verge of being taken advantage of.

Appraisal vs. Home Inspection

The simplest way to look at it is this. An appraisal tells you how much your home is worth. A home inspection tells you what is wrong with your home. A home inspection is ONLY focused on the condition of the home, and the appraisal looks at condition as part of a bigger picture which takes into account many other variable factors.

It is important to note that an appraisal also discloses the overall condition of the subject property, but it is not in the same way as the home inspection does. You are 100% better off going with a comprehensive home inspection if you want to know the real truth and history of the actual physical house itself.

Myths and Realities: Real Estate Appraisals

Throughout the years I have come across many homebuyers who have been told many half-truths about appraisal values. The list below is a compilation of the most outrageous myths about appraisals I have heard over the years:

- **Myth:** The town assessment is the same as market value.
  Reality: No way, no how! The difference between the two is night and day. The assessed value is most often two years behind and more importantly is intentionally less than the market value of the home. By the way, the assessment is a drive by which completely misses the entire inside features, amenities and details of the inside.

- **Myth:** The home value in the appraisal for the buyer is different than the appraised value of the seller.
  Reality: They should both be the same. In a perfect world all appraisers should have an objective interest in performing the appraisal without regard to the financial intention of either party. The reality is that we would not be in the mess we are in if appraisers would have been more objective when appraising homes.

- **Myth:** Replacement cost and market value is pretty much the same.
  Reality: No. Replacement cost is how much it would cost to rebuild your house from the ground up in the event of a catastrophic event that utterly destroyed it. Not to sound repetitive, but market value is based on what the other homes similar to yours in your area are selling for.

- **Myth:** Don't appraisers just come up with a simple formula which automatically calculates the home value?
  Reality: No. There are many variables that factor into the home value such as homes that have sold in your neighborhood, square footage, overall condition of home and many other factors.

- **Myth:** When the whole neighborhood is going up in value then any home in that neighborhood should be going up in value.
  Reality: Not exactly. While the homes that have sold in your neighborhood play a huge role in your home value there are specific traits that are unique to each individual property. By the way, those same individual traits are the same ones that prevent your home from plummeting in value when your neighbors sell their home to their son for thousands less than the market value supports.

- **Myth:** It is easy to tell what a home is worth by looking at the outside.
- **Reality:** Not even a little bit. Yes, you can gain some insight into the mind of the previous owner, but there is no way to tell what a house is worth by looking on the outside. Once again there are many factors that go into calculating the value and outside appearance is just one of them.

- **Myth:** If you pay for the appraisal you own it.
  Reality: No. The appraisal is owned by the lender. The only legal responsibility the lender has is to give you a copy of your appraisal. No more. No less.

- **Myth:** You do not need to be concerned with the nitty-gritty details of the appraisal as long as the value comes in good enough.
  Reality: Wrong! You need to review your appraisal to verify all of the facts about the house, and you may also uncover some facts that you did not know.

CHAPTER 11

Creating Your Foreclosure "Dream Team": Home Inspectors

There are many reasons why you should get a home inspection, and each one of them are valid. I will list a few that are very important. Home inspections not only verify major things such as making sure that the roof does not have leaks or rotted wood, but home inspections also verify that the home systems are working properly and verifies if the foundation your prospective home is built on is stable or crumbling.

In other words, a home inspection is simply when a licensed home inspector does a visual and functional test and observation of all the parts of the house from top to bottom, including all the systems of the house. A home inspection tells you if everything in the house is working as it should be.

A traditional home inspection will give you the details about the heating and cooling systems, electrical and plumbing systems; floors, walls, the roof, ceilings, doors and windows, the home's foundation and the structural parts of the house, including the basement.

99.9% of Mortgage Lenders Do Not Require Home Inspections

Mortgage lenders do not require you to get a home inspection before they lend you money. Lenders make their decision based on the appraisal, which gives them the value of the home. However, I have seen times when the appraiser noted things on his report that needed to be fixed and upgraded, and as a consequence the lender then asked for the home to be inspected. However, as a rule of thumb, if you are investing in foreclosures, you will want to know as much as humanly possible about your prospective investment.

But I have Lived Here My Whole Life!

Mark wisely chose to be quiet as Donna verbally kicked the crap out of their appraiser about the many things he did not say was wrong with the house on the appraisal. After enduring the first two years of marriage, Mark had learned that when Donna had her mind made up, it was best to let her vent her frustration.

However, the issue was that Donna's argument had two problems. The first problem was that she mistakenly assumed that the appraiser would check for holes and cracks in the foundation, termites in the walls and mold under the hardwood floors. The second problem was that she had lived in the house for the last thirty years and *she* did not even know about the cracks in the foundation right next to the washer and dryer she used weekly.

After twenty minutes of taking one of the worst verbal beatings that a person could receive, the appraiser finally managed to blurt out, "For goodness sakes woman. I am an appraiser...not a home inspector! Pay the $400 and get your inspection done!"

Mark wondered why it had taken him more than twenty minutes to defend himself with the truth about what he already knew. A home inspection would easily have caught all the problems Donna pointed out to the appraiser.

Why You Absolutely, Positively Need A Home Inspection When Investing In Foreclosures!

It is just good ole' fashion common sense. If you are buying a home, would you want to know if everything is working as it should? What good does it do you to negotiate a great deal on the purchase price, but after moving into your new home you realize that the sellers were willing to go as low as they did because of all the problems the house has? A home inspection can also give you the leverage for negotiating for costly repairs to be corrected before agreeing on a final purchase price.

Even if you have bought ten houses and have a ton of real life experience and knowledge, you still need a home inspector. The only exception is if you are a licensed home inspector and have all of the tools and training, then you get a pass on this one. There are crucial pieces of knowledge and know-how that only an experienced home inspector will be able to pick up on.

A home inspector not only knows how and why things works, but he or she will know why things do not work and what has to be done to fix it.

The other important point is that as a buyer it is hard and difficult to stay level-headed and detached from the emotional part of buying a home. No matter how much you try, if you find out a vital piece of information that the home seller did not disclose, it is usually perceived as being deceptive, regardless if the home sellers knew about it or not.

Home Grade: Pass or Fail?

It is not possible for a home to fail a home inspection. A home inspector just tells you what is right and what is wrong and needs repairs based on the home as it is today. It is not like with the appraisal where you actually need it to come in for a certain value in order to get the mortgage. It is also not a code inspection to make sure the house is up to code according to town laws. All the home inspection does is provide detailed information about the physical condition and systems of the house.

How To Hire An Home Inspector

Just like when ordering your appraisal, the home inspection will most likely be done by your real estate agent or mortgage professional. However, many foreclosure investors have more input into hiring a home inspector than with an appraiser. Even with that being said, the real estate agent and mortgage profession will usually coordinate the hiring of a home inspector for your prospective home.

If you do find yourself being the one responsible for finding, interviewing and ultimately hiring your home inspector, then you will want to make sure you follow the same three-step formula you used for finding a real estate agent, attorney and mortgage professional.

The True Cost of A Home Inspection

The cost of a home inspection for an average single family home will be different depending on the types of tests you want performed. As a good rule of thumb, you should be prepared to spend anywhere from five to six hundred dollars to get all of the testing done.

Yes, that is a lot of money; however, do you know how much it costs to replace a septic system? Or how much it costs to upgrade an electrical system? At the end of the day you need to know any and every possible thing that can go right or wrong with the home BEFORE you buy the home. Being able to sleep at night knowing that you have made a good decision is worth many more times the cost of a home inspection. Trust me, because I know from personal experience.

The other factor which makes the cost well worth the investment, is that a home inspection with a single family home in average condition only takes about three to four hours, and sometimes can take up to half the day. Now let's do the math: Three to six hours to save tens of thousands of dollars and years of aggravation. Where do I sign-up? Also, if the house is smaller or is brand new, then the inspection usually is done in a shorter time frame than if it is an older home with many different electrical and plumbing systems. It may also take longer if you are asking the home inspector questions about each step of the process while he's in the home. Which I recommend, by the way!

The most important point to remember is that you are not paying the inspector by the hours, but you are paying him for a complete and comprehensive report about the condition of the foreclosure. You are paying him for his experience, education, knowledge about homes, and his overall competence. It is also of the utmost importance that you go with the home inspector and listen, ask questions and take notes.

Preparing For Your Home Inspection

You, the home inspector, the seller and maybe both real estate agents will be at the home inspection. However, regardless of who else shows up, it should definitely be you, the home inspector and seller. You should be glued to the inspector the entire time he or she is in the home, because the more eyeballs looking things over the better chance for any little detail to be reviewed. Here are some do's and don'ts when preparing to go to the inspection:

- Bring pen, paper and a list of issues your preliminary research turned up, as well as the seller's disclosure, so that the home inspector can address those issues while there.

- Bring a camera and video recorder because it is important to document what you like, so you can objectively evaluate it when you are home.

- Dress comfortably because you could be crawling in attics, underneath houses and battling through an occasional cobweb.

- By the way, DO NOT bring kids to the home inspection because they could prevent you from paying one hundred percent attention to what is going on, or they could get hurt.

SURPRISE!!!
Do not be too surprised when you get the results of the home inspection. Regardless of the condition of the home, every home inspection reveals something that no one knew about the house. It is normal and to be expected.

Rules of Conduct For Your Home Inspection

Now that I have told why you need a home inspection and advised you on the wisdom of attending, I will take some time to point out that it is important to be respectful of the home sellers when inspecting the home. Observe the following:

- Have special consideration for elderly sellers and tenants. Realize the sellers could have possibly raised multiple generations of their family in the home or suffered a death of a loved one.
- Honor the sellers feeling by keeping sarcastic or negative comments to yourself…at least while at the home.
- Do not go through personal stuff while there. Stick to the systems and components that the home inspector is observing.
- Wipe your feet before walking in.
- Be mindful of pets escaping outside.
- Do not touch anything that looks valuable or fragile. If you do not know about something, then do not touch it!
- Find at least one thing to compliment the home seller about.

Who Gets A Copy of the Home Inspection?

This is one of the major differences from the appraisal, because the home inspector gives you the original report and you determine who receives a copy. However, you should be very careful about who gets a copy of the home inspection report because I have seen a number of tricks that sellers have done to buyers in order to get a higher selling price.

For example:

- The seller uses the buyer's copy of the home inspection as leverage against the buyers' offering price.
- The seller intentionally understates or minimizes costly or dangerous property conditions.

Always remember that you as the buyer have the irrevocable right to receive the home inspection and determine who gets the information and when they receive it.

However, there are some findings in the home inspection which absolutely should be disclosed to everyone ASAP. This is especially true when there is a dangerous or immediate threatening situation such as a gas leak or a faulty leaking septic tank.

How to read your home inspection report

Here is the quick and cheat sheet for reading and understanding the home inspection report by breaking it apart into these categories:

- **Necessary expenses:** These are the items which you must get repaired or updated in order to make the home livable.

- **Dangerous:** Any type of exposed wiring, broken guardrails, missing steps, etc.

- **Damage Causing Parts:** These are components which are causing damage and ongoing damage to the home.

- **Non-working Parts:** All the things that are not working properly or maybe not working at all.

- **Repairs That Can Be Deferred:** These are repairs that you might want to see done, but they are not necessary for the home to be livable.

- **Anything else:** These are the miscellaneous repairs that you may want to see done at some later date to improve the overall look of your home. The house will not fall apart if these things are not done, but it would definitely make it nicer to live there.

It is important to separate the information in the home inspection report in this manner, because it is easy to get overwhelmed when seeing a home inspection for the first time. In fact, if your best friend handed you a home inspection report for a brand new home and asked you for your opinion on whether or not they should buy it you could probably say yes or no, solely based on the not-so-positive information included in EVERY home inspection report. It is important to keep this in mind when reviewing your report.

What To Watch Out For When Reading Your Inspection

In the previous section I gave you some categories to break your home inspection information into in order to make it easy-to-understand. However, there are some potential landmines hidden within home inspections, such as:

- **The hidden in plain sight release permission check box -** There are some home inspection agreements that have a little check box which states that the inspector can release the home inspection report to any and all third parties without additional permission from the buyer. The reason why some home inspectors do this is to solicit business from real estate agents and other real estate professionals involved in the process. However, it can be used to give the sellers access to the report upon their request.

- **Who will be the first to see the report once it is completed? -** This goes hand in hand with the hidden check box in the example above. If the home inspector releases it to the seller's agent first, then how do you think they will use it? Of course they will try to negotiate a higher selling price. That is why you must make sure that you are the first person to receive it and the one who controls who sees it.

- **What you were told at the inspection is different than what is in the report -** There are some inspectors who will tell you one thing and then write a totally different piece of information in the report. If you were told something, then the report should reflect the exact same piece of information.

When To Get Additional Specialized Inspections

There may be times when your standard home inspection may not be enough. This is more common when the standard inspection turns up some facts which need further investigation. You should consider hiring additional specialists if:

- Your inspector says you should because he noticed some major issues in one of the homes major systems.

- You have a sensitivity or allergic reaction to certain chemicals, materials or temperature.

- You feel the home inspection report neglected to cover an issue which you viewed as important to you.

- There are unique features to the house, such as an attached dock with a boat house, a older septic tank, or in-ground swimming pool.

- The seller's disclosure mentioned some conditions which warrant further investigation.

Why You Should Get A Home Inspection When You're Bidding on A Newly Built Home

When you buy new construction or have a home custom built you have an expectation of receiving a home that is in mint-condition, and that is quite a reasonable request. However, the reality is sometimes very different than the expectation. Let me give you some examples of issues you could have with a newly built home:

- **Building code violations** – usually occurs in the form of loose wires, pipes that aren't long enough or improper heights on fixtures and outlets.

- **Improper ventilation issues** – the most common problem areas are the attic, roof and kitchen, which creates mold issues.

- **Roof problems** – sometimes inferior shingles are used and are not nailed down properly.

- **Incorrect weather detailing** – creates drafts or leaks which drive up your heating and cooling bill.

- **Uneven land, improper water main connections or incorrectly connected sewer lines**

CHAPTER 12

Creating Your Foreclosure "Dream Team": Home Improvement Contractors

In many cases, the success or failure of a foreclosure hinges upon whether or not you can get the house into a livable or sellable condition in a short amount of time. If you have the skills, tools and expertise to make the repairs yourself, then you are all set, but many people need outside help to get a house in good condition. If that describes you, then I strongly suggest having a system in place to find, hire and manage home improvement contractors to avoid a very painful lesson later on.

One of the simplest ways to go about the process of managing home contractors is using the bidding process and the pay-as-you-go method. This simply means that you will interview multiple contractors and ask them to submit a bid for the work you want done, and then set up a payment schedule to pay them in small installments until the work is completed. This way, both you and the contractor are protected and guaranteed to get the best out of the working relationship. As a foreclosure buyer, your main goals are to have quality work performed on time and at the agreed upon price. From the contractor's perspective, he wants to do the work that is well spelled out and be paid in an ongoing and consistent manner. The system I recommend accomplishes all those goals for both you and the contractor.

The Key To Successfully Working With A Home Improvement Contractor

Over the years, I have noticed that many foreclosure buyers immediately think that home contractors are out to screw them over. In most cases this is absolutely NOT true. Home improvement contractors are normal hard-working people just like you and me and can often find you bargains and deals if you treat them with dignity and respect. In fact, the key to successfully working with contractors depends on your ability to lay out a plan for the work you want done and how the contractor will be paid in a detail oriented way.

Before you even begin to think about hiring a contractor to do work on your property, you should know exactly what you want and how much you have to spend to get it. The best way to do this is to simply grab a pencil and paper and walk through the property and make a list of repairs that you know you want. Secondly, review the home inspection report and appraisal to find out the exact repairs that are required by law. You can also use this information to discover repairs that could be made to dramatically impact the property value. If you want to add an extra layer of security to your renovation project, you can also hire a structural engineer to give you more input on improvements that can be made. However, in most cases the appraisal and home inspection will provide more than enough information to keep your mind and wallet busy for a long time.

Step #1: Preparing Your Work/Bid Worksheet

The best way to organize your thoughts and the information you are getting from the appraisal and home inspection is to use a worksheet that you write your requests on. This works best because it allows you to keep track of all the work you want done and gives you an overview of the bids from all the different contractors you contacted.

The worksheet does not have to be complicated or twenty pages, but it does have to clearly spell out the work that you are requesting to be completed. Secondly, you must use one worksheet per room. For example, if you are having work done to three bedrooms, two bathrooms and the living room, then you should have six different work/bid worksheets. This makes it really easy for you to understand, and easy for the contractors to understand, as well.

The first step is to create a worksheet for each room that you want completed. Then you should complete a worksheet to compare each contracting quote you receive. This can be as simple as having a column for contractors name, project cost and time quote. This will be your tracking sheet so you can get the important information at a glance. Below, you have an example of a bid worksheet:

Work Specification Worksheet	
Bedroom #2	**Price**
Dimensions:	$_____
Wall Covering:	$_____
Painting:	$_____
Flooring:	$_____
Closets:	$_____
Windows:	$_____
Spackling:	$_____
Electrical:	$_____
Lighting Fixtures:	$_____
Heating:	$_____
Room Entry Door:	$_____
Additional Repairs:	$_____
Total Price for Entire Job	$_____
Estimated Time To Complete The Work Quoted Above	$_____

Step #2: Finding A Contractor

Once you have clearly defined the work that you want done to your home, you should turn your attention to finding a contractor. The guidelines for selecting a contractor use the same formula for selecting each of your real estate professionals.

1. Select at least three local home improvement companies to talk with.

2. Preferably, one of the above should be a referral from a friend, family member or co-worker that has worked with the company.

3. Ask for a specific person to work with, then meet with them to discuss your goals and see if there is a good fit.

This simple formula for finding a good home improvement contractor has been successfully used by thousands of foreclosure bargain buyers, so it will definitely work for you.

Step 3: Interviewing The Home Improvement Contractors

Selecting the right contractor is an important step when you are investing in a foreclosure, so here are some questions you will want to ask:

- **Are you licensed?**
  This is a basic question you should never skip. There are many contractors who are not licensed, but people falsely assume they are. If a contractor is not licensed, then you are at risk of being sued without having any legal recourse.

- **Are you insured?**
  This question is in the same category as the licensure question. In fact, you should never hire a contractor who does not have the proper license. If someone gets hurt while working on your house you could be held legally responsible.

Also, check and verify if your homeowners insurance offers any coverage for workers or renovations.

- **How long have you been licensed?**
  You also want to make sure that you are not dealing with a contractor who just became aware of the newest guidelines and technologies for working on your home. You want a seasoned veteran.

- **How many years have you been doing home renovations?**
  Renovating your foreclosure is a time when you cannot afford to be a guinea pig. You want someone who has many years of experience.

- **Have you ever done the same type of work as I need to be completed?**
  Be sure to ask the contractor if he has done the specific type of work that you need. Just because he has repaired hundreds of roofs, does not mean he is a expert on repairing foundations.

- **What is your niche or specialty?**
  You should always choose a specialist over a contractor who does a little bit of everything. When it comes to home repairs, there is no substitute for expertise.

- **Do you have any other projects that you are currently working on? If so, can I visit a current work site?**
  A reputable contractor will be able to easily give you references and other job site locations for you to visit. The only exception to this rule is if the contractor does not currently have any other homes he is currently working on.

- **Will you be hiring subcontractors for my job?**
  Most contractors hire subcontractors to work their home repair jobs. This is the standard industry practice; however, you may want to take a small amount of time to meet everyone working on your home.

- **Will you be able to provide documentation that all the contractors you hire will also be licensed and insured?**
  It is also very important to make sure that subcontractors are also insured and licensed. If an accident were to occur and cause harm, you will be just as liable for a subcontractor as you are for a contractor.

- **How long will it take for you to complete the work that I need done?**
  This may seem obvious, but sometimes homeowners get so excited about the process that they forget to ask upfront how long it will take for the work to be completed. Then, they are weeks into a project before they remember to get a more realistic timeline of the work to be completed.

Once you have interviewed your prospective contractors, then you should make a decision on which one you would like to work with. Always be sure to consider whether or not you personally like the contractor, their current workload, and the amount of time it would take for them to complete the project.

Step 4: Paying The Contractor

There are several ways homeowners have traditionally paid contractors. However, there is only way you should pay a contractor to prevent any type of problems or hard feelings. Here are several possible options for paying a contractor:

1. 100% of the payment up front.
2. 50% to start and 50% when the job is completed.
3. 1/3 paid up front, 1/3 paid at the mid-point of the project and 1/3 paid at the completion of the project.
4. Payments made at some pre-arranged milestones.

While all of these are payment options, the best method to pay your contractor is to pay each week for the work done the previous week. So, for example you would have your contractor perform work Monday through Friday. On Friday he would submit the work completed and costs based on your bid specification worksheet, then you would walk through the property to check the work for quality and completeness. Once you are satisfied, then you write him a check for the work completed.

CHAPTER 13

7 Steps To Becoming An Instant Foreclosure Expert

When you buy a home that is listed on the MLS, there is some inherent risk involved. You must verify the ownership history, insurance claims history and other things like the size of the property. However, when you are buying a foreclosure property, the risk involved multiplies several times over. In this chapter, I reveal the top seven ways for you to check and make sure the foreclosure bargain you buy is in good condition, in a decent neighborhood and will provide a profitable investment for you.

Whenever you buy a foreclosure, your ability to get to the truth quickly is much more important than when buying a traditional listing. In fact, if you sign a purchase and sales agreement, slap down your hard earned money and then find out the house is a complete and utter disaster next door to the worst serial sex offender in the history of the state, it does not matter how good of a deal you just bought, because you are up a creek with a paddle the size of a plastic spoon.

Now here is an overview of the seven steps to get the insider truth on any property you are thinking about buying:

Step #1 – Search sex offender registry
Step #2 – Ask for the seller's disclosure form
Step #3 – Visit the property at least four different times
Step #4 – Drive around your target neighborhood
Step #5 – Research at the local government offices
Step #6 – Inspect the inside of the house
Step #7 – Inspect the outside of the house

These steps have been compiled after many years of watching homebuyers make mistake after mistake. Follow these steps and you can rest assured that you will know just as much about the house and neighborhood as the current owners know.

Step #1: Search The State And National Registry For Known Sex Offenders Living In The Prospective Neighborhood

This has to be the most often over-looked first step that foreclosure buyers forget to do. And do not even think about telling me you do not have children because everyone has…

…nieces
…nephews
…visiting friends or family with children
…spouse or significant other.

The real question you should be asking is, "When will your loved one come by for a visit?" Without a doubt this is the most important first step you should take when considering a home.

Once you have the information, the choice is then yours to decide whether or not you want to proceed forward with living in a neighborhood with one or many known sex offenders. To complete a search for sex offenders go to www.google.com and enter "sex offender's database" for your state, and you will have several links to online databases.

Step #2: Ask for seller's disclosure statement

The second thing you should do if you are buying a pre-foreclosure, auction sold or bank-owned property is ask for the seller's disclosure statement from either your real estate agent, auction committee or the sellers themselves. The seller's disclosure is a form that is required by law which lets you know the following:

- **Title** – reveals any issues or disputes against the ownership of the sellers. It is also a written and legal document with the seller's claiming to be the true owners and thus have the legal right to sell the property.
- **Structure** – covers all code violations for any reason on the entire property.

- **Land** – reveals if the home sits on a fault line, flood zone or unstable earth foundation.
- **Environment** – has there been any problems with nearby businesses, construction or homes that would pose an environmental threat.
- **Homeowner's Association** – reveals if the owner has additional monthly payments for any other type of service that is provided in relation to the home.
- **Plumbing** – discloses the condition, location and general condition of the system
- **Appliances** – covers if there have been issues with the gas, electricity and functionality of any appliances included in the sale.
- **Heating and air conditioning systems** – gives you an insight into what can cause major issues in one of the major home systems.
- **Other & Additional** – discloses everything else like pest problems, damaged roof or incomplete construction etc.

Beware Seller's Disclosure

While getting a seller's disclosure as early in the process as possible is usually advisable, you should take it with a grain of salt. Most rookie foreclosure buyers stop researching as soon as they receive the seller's disclosure. This is a HUGE mistake. You should use the seller's disclosure as a guide, but never as the final authority.

Step #3: Visit the property AT LEAST four times

There is no way you should even consider buying a home until you have looked at it several times at different hours of day and night. You will not be able to get a good feeling for the area without doing this step.

You will want to see the home at the worst hours because you will be living there twenty four seven, three hundred and sixty five days a year. The next visit after the initial visit should be a weeknight and you should be looking for proper street lighting, flow of traffic, suspicious looking characters.

Then you should visit it during the day and night on a weekend because that is when you will have a chance to really hit the goldmine of information by meeting the neighbors.

Step #4: Walk & Drive Through The Surrounding Neighborhood

One of the greatest sources of information you will ever come across in your search for information, is the neighbors of the particular house you are interested in. The neighbors will know how often the previous homeowners upgraded the exterior of the home, how they maintained the yard and their overall pride of ownership.

The best way to "bump" into the neighbors is to go for a nice evening walk in the neighborhood to see if anyone is outside doing yard work or playing with the kids. If you find someone, simply spark up a conversation stating that you are thinking about moving into the neighborhood and what has their experience been like.

During the conversation be sure to get specific about the house you are interested in. For example, some good questions to ask are:

- How long did or have the owners lived there?

- If you could do it over again, would you choose the same neighborhood?

- Have there been any major renovations on the house recently?

- How did they take care of the house over the years?

- Have there been any crimes committed in the house?

- Are there things that happen at certain times of year that are noticeable?

I would even suggest asking the neighbors about the previous owners prior to the current owners. If they have the contact information then you should ask for it. No one will know as much about the house as someone who has lived in it over an extended period of time. The point is to ask as many questions as possible because that is the only way to get as many answers as you need to make an intelligent decision.

The neighbors will also be able to give you a good feel of the general attitude of the community. Are they friendly or standoffish? Is the neighborhood mostly comprised of renters or older people? Is there an informal or formal neighborhood association? Those type of questions and observations reveal tons of information about the neighborhood.

Waiting behind a school bus while it is dropping off kids in the morning might not seem like a big deal when you first go to visit the property, but it will be a completely different story when you are stuck behind a school bus for an extra fifteen minutes every morning when you are leaving for work. In order to really observe the traffic patterns, you must first visit the property in the morning when schools are starting and in the afternoon when schools are letting out and parents are coming home from work.

That is the best way to get the inside scoop on traffic patterns. Do not minimize this step because it seems trivial. By the way, when you are walking the neighborhood you should also be looking for school crossing signs, school bus stops, traffic lights and stop signs. It is also a good idea to call up the police station and ask them if there have been a lot of issues with speeding in the neighborhood or on the street.

When you are walking around the neighborhood you should also be watching out for any type of contractors sign on homes or in the yards. Jot down the number because you will definitely want to call up these folks and ask them about the home, area or general take on the neighborhood.

Imagine knowing in advance that several people on the same side of the street have hired someone to repair their home's foundation in the last several months. That could possibly mean there is some type of earth movement beneath the street. Or you could even possibly find out who did home repairs on the home you are thinking about buying. That would be a huge bonus, but you will never know if you do not take the time to write down the numbers and call them up.

Just like with the neighbors, if you let them know you are considering purchasing in the area and need some background information they will be just as inquisitive about you as a potential customer as you are about the prospective home.

Step # 5 Researching At Local Government Level

During the course of your house investigation you will need to purchase manila folders to contain all of the various copies and research you turn up on the property. It should be your number one goal to get copies of every piece of information the city department will allow you to. This is important because your detective work will require you to visit several, if not all, of the following places, and it is very unlikely that you will remember all of this stuff in your head.

The major offices you should visit in person or online are:

- Tax Assessors Office (Tax Collector and City or Town Clerk)
- Building Department (also known as Code Enforcement)
- Planning & Zoning Department
- Public Works Department

Tax Assessors Office

The tax assessor's office is the first place you should visit because it will give you an idea of how the city actually views the property you are considering. This is very important because the tax assessor will determine how the property is valued and consequently taxed.

When visiting the tax assessor's office you are looking for the following information:

Current and previous ownership history
- Ownership deed
- Sale prices
- Sale dates
- Land area
- Lot frontage
- Zoning class
- Available utilities
- Assessor's tax map

Building construction details
- Heating
- Electrical
- Plumbing
- Date of construction
- Permit numbers
  - Dates of remodeling
  - Renovations performed
  - Building size
  - Sketches with measurements
- Room counts
- Other building features / amenities
- References to other site / subdivision plans
- Any other additional notes and comments
- Tax Rate (or Mill Rate)

While gathering this information you will want to keep your eyes out for information that will give you insight into:

- Real estate tax history for the property
- Overall real estate tax trends
- Most recent full assessment
- How they calculate assessed value

- Are there any city wide contract negotiations underway which could impact real estate taxes such as Police, Fire or Teacher Union contracts?

You will also want to know what major highway or road and public utilities projects are on the horizon that could possibly impact real estate taxes.

Not knowing about major construction projects can result in being completely side-blinded when your taxes increase by over 50%, like they recently did in a town near me. There were homeowners whose taxes went from $3,200 per year to over $4,800 a year. Talk about lifestyle adjustment!

Building Department

This is where you will find out things such as if they made any legal changes to the property. When walking in be sure to let them know that you are contemplating buying a certain property and want to do your homework. By the way, it is possible for them not to have information on a property because nothing has been done. And then there are other times when you will need a trash bag to hold all of the paperwork. It just depends.

The Building Department for a home could contain:

- Previous requests for renovation permits
- The actual permit approvals or denials
- Lot line disputes or changes
- Future construction plans
- Floor plans
- Previous inspections
- Violations
- Requests or denials for zoning variances

It is also a good idea to get the contact information for the contractor's names on the permits because they will be a good source of information for potential issues.

Planning & Zoning Department

One of the most worrisome and troubling times as a homeowner is when your neighborhood is being rezoned to allow for business and developments. Trust me when I tell you that construction projects can dramatically alter your lifestyle. By the way, usually there is nothing you can do to stop this from happening.

Every town, city, community and village goes through this type of transition. My goal is to provide you with the tools to see it coming and not be taken by surprise. The way to find out this information is by actually going over the master plan that the city has for your neighborhood. Each city has one of those big life-size maps in their planning and zoning office, which clearly outlines the next five to ten years worth of developments for everyone to see. You will want to look to see what subdivisions, businesses or general construction projects are slated for your area.

The planning and zoning ordinances will clearly spell out each owner's lot, yard size and type of property that can be built in certain areas. Zoning changes can have such a huge impact on your life, so you will want to know the following:

- Is the house you are considering zoned for residential use?
- Is a different zoning area next to the property?
- Is the property in two different zones?
- What are the minimum lot requirements?

You will also want to make sure that you know if your property is legally non-conforming or grandfathered in. Legal non-conforming means that the house was constructed before the current zoning plans were in place.

Registry of Deeds/Courthouse

The courthouse or registry of deeds is where you will find the technical and exact legal description of the property. It will detail the following:

- Legal right-of-ways to neighboring properties
- Streets that may appear on maps but do not actually exist
- Legal rights to common areas around the property
- Neighborhood sanitary systems
- Any type of land exceptions for preservation and conservation

Pumping Utility Companies For Information

This next little tip I am about to share with you is one that 99.9% of homebuyers have never even thought of. It involves actually calling the utility companies with the home address of the property you are investigating and asking for annual cost or average monthly usage. If the usage is high then it can indicate that there is a problem in the area with electrical lines, inefficient insulation, water pressure problems etc.

Step #6: Inspecting The Outside Of The House

Now it is time to look at the exterior of the house and see how it measures up to your taste and research information. It is very important that in this phase you guard your expressions, feelings and thoughts until you are out of the presence of the sellers and their agent.

The major things that you are looking for are:

Foundation
- Do you notice any cracks?
- Are there any repaired cracks?

Roof
- Do you observe any tree sap or mold on the roof?
- Is there any sagging anywhere?
- Where are the vents or chimney?
- Do you see any lifted or curled shingles?
- Are there multiple layers of shingles?

Siding
- What is the material made of?
- Does it look old and worn out?
- Can you actually get a paint chip or color type?
- Does the wood look like it is peeling or splintering apart?
- Do you see the right type of caulking?
- Do you observe mold?

Trim (shadow boards, and overhangs)
- Is the trim complete or is some absent?
- Is the paint peeling?
- Do you see broken, rotted or cracked trim?

Windows
- Are there any missing, cracked or broken?
- What type of material are the windows made of?
- Are the windows insulated?
- Do you see storm windows?

Doors
- What type of material are the doors made of?
- Are they stained or painted?

Every house will have different construction and materials, but what you are looking for is to see the general condition and to make sure that you have every piece of information that you need to make an informed decision.

Step #7: Inspecting the Inside of The House

This is only possible with pre-foreclosure and bank-owned homes; however, when possible this is the time where all your homework pays off. You will be able to point out any difference between what the sellers or banks are telling you, and what the city says they have.

If you do not know where to begin, here are some questions to open up the conversation (Yes, you may already know the answers, but you are just trying to get the ball rolling) Here are some sample questions to ask the sellers if you are purchasing a pre-foreclosure:

- When did you buy the property?
- When did you put the house on the market?
- Have you already selected another place to live? If so, when do you have to be there?
- When are you planning on moving?
- What type of work have you done to the house since buying it?
- Did you do the work yourself or contract it out?
- Do you have the contractors contact information?
- Was the contractors work guaranteed for a period of time? If so, how long?
- Did you get the permits from the town to do the work?
- Have you ever been required to file an insurance claim due to damage?
  - o If so, what was it and who repaired it?

The following are places you should look within the house:

Floors
- How old are the floorboards
- Gaps between boards
- Split boards
- Cracked tiles
- Cracked and missing grout between tiles or along wall and baseboards
- Are there any diagonal cracks above doors and windows?
- Do floors sag
- Do floors have spring in them
- Do floors squeak or creak

Bathrooms
- Check around the toilet and tub/shower for soft or spongy flooring.
- Flush the toilet to check pressure.

- Lift the tank cover and check to see if the flush valve is new or old.
- Watch for leaks around base of bowl.
- Check water connections for age and corrosion
- Run water in tubs and sinks to check for possible blocked drains
- Faucets
- Is there any dripping after you shut off the water?
- Check all water connections for age and corrosion
- Is there a strong, vortex flow down the drain or does the water seem to drain slowly
- Do the owners know if their water is hard or soft? Water described as "hard" is high in dissolved minerals, specifically calcium and magnesium.

Heating, Cooling and Electrical Systems

It is very important that you know and recognize that the major systems in the house are very expensive to replace and repair, so you need to get the contact information of any contractor, company or service man that has done work on the house.

- Test all the light switches
- Are the lights flickering, which indicate the fuses may have too many circuits
- Do you see any ceiling fans?
- Do you hear any humming noises when you turn switches on?
- What type of heating system does the house use?
- How often have the sellers changed the filters?
- What type of fuel does the heating system use?
- If oil or propane is used, where are the fuel storage tanks?
- If electric heat, is it baseboard or radiant?
- What is the age of the heating system?
- Is there any central cooling system?
- What size is it?
- Does it adequately cool the entire home?

- How old is it?

Kitchen Appliances
- Do all the appliances work without any problems whatsoever?
- How old are the appliances?
- Have they ever required servicing?

Doors, Windows, and Cabinets
- Do all doors and windows open to the extent you would expect?
- Do any stick?
- Do any not open all the way?
- Do any stay closed?
- Do all of the locks and latches function, as they should?
- Is there any cabinet hardware missing?
- Do all kitchen drawers slide in an out smoothly?
- Are there any that have broken drawer slides?
- Are there any doors missing doorstops, which would allow the doorknob to smash into the wall when opened?

General Storage
- Does each bedroom have a closet?
- Is there a linen closet?
- Is there a pantry?
- Is there a utility closet?
- Do the closets have ample depth?
- Do the closets have ample shelving?

Basement
- Are there shut-offs for all the water lines/supplies?
- If you end up buying the house, BE SURE to have the seller show you where all the shut-offs are.
- Is any part of the basement finished?
- Does the basement feel damp?
- Does the basement look damp?

- If you can see any sections of the foundation, do you see any cracks?

Attic
- Ask if there is an attic and how it is accessed
- Check for any signs of dampness, rodent infestation or overall shabby conditions

CHAPTER 14

Financing Your Foreclosure:
Secrets, Tips, and Strategies

This chapter will give you a detailed look at the entire mortgage process. It will also serve as a step-by-step plan to help you get the best and lowest interest rate possible when buying your foreclosure. There is immense value within the next several pages, so be sure to get a pen, paper or write within the pages as certain things are sure to stick out. Just by reading these pages you will be more than prepared to finance your foreclosure and attend your meeting with your mortgage professional with confidence. It is also the time when you realize the benefits of all your reading books, saving money and hours of hard work.

In all of the foreclosure investing strategies that I have discussed in this book, I always began with you getting pre-approved for a mortgage. This also includes having your deposit or down payment money arranged well in advance of beginning.

So with that in mind, let's go back to school. Except this time the name of the school is Mortgage University.

Everything You Ever Wanted To Know About Mortgages...And Then Some

We will start with the basics. A mortgage is when a bank loans you money to buy a house. The word mortgage is also interchangeable with the phrase home loan. Now as you can imagine, no one except maybe your immediate family is in the business of loaning (or sometimes giving) money away without expecting a return on their investment. Therefore banks charge interest on their loans as wells as numerous fees and points. A point is one percentage point of the total loan amount. ($200,000 x .01 = $2,000)

The Two Types of Mortgages

No matter how creative bankers get, the fact of the matter is, there are only two types of mortgages; fixed or adjustable. You can further break those two down into various types of fixed and adjustable, but the essence always remains the same.

Once you separate fixed mortgages from adjustable mortgages, you can then break them down even further. The first variation is called conventional or conforming mortgages. The second variation is called government insured mortgages. Therefore, you can have fixed conventional mortgages or adjustable conventional mortgages.

Conventional means that the borrower and the mortgage amount falls within a specific set of guidelines and requires putting down a substantial down payment. Regular banks where you do your normal checking and savings usually offer conventional mortgages, but there are also conventional mortgage lenders. The guidelines for conventional or conforming mortgages tend to be strict and unforgiving when it comes to lower credit scores or a small amount of savings available to use for your down payment and closing costs.

Government insured loans means that the U.S. Housing and Urban Development Program (HUD) offers a federal insurance program which provides extra protection against default for the mortgage lenders. These programs include Federal Housing Authority (FHA), Veterans Administration (VA) and U.S. Department of Agriculture Rural Development (USDA) loans.

It is much simpler to think of all mortgages as fixed or adjustable so that you can keep the insanity out of your mind. I have given you the major terms, phrases and definitions that you need to know to make an informed decision. If you are similar to me, then you do not want to worry about the dozens of variations of these two types of mortgages.

So, here is a simple guide to help you:

1. **Fixed Mortgages** – Includes 50, 40, 30, 25, 20, 15 or 10 year term periods. With fixed mortgages you always make the same payment each month. You just choose how long you

want to be paying the same payment. There are also fixed balloon mortgages which are fixed for a period of time but then require you to make a lump sum payment all at one time at the end of the loan term. Balloon mortgages are pretty scary…even from a mortgage professional's point of view.

2. **Adjustable Rate Mortgages (ARM)** – These mortgages do just what their name implies – adjust. You may have a fixed payment for one month, one year or ten years, but at some point they will adjust. What the mortgage lenders do to come up with an adjustable mortgage rate is borrow money from huge global banks such as the London Interbank Offer Rater (LIBOR), the 11th Federal Home Loan Bank District Costs of Funds (COFI), U.S. Treasury Bills, or Certificates of Deposit (CDs). Whatever the interest rate those global banks charge the mortgage lenders is referred to as the *index*. The mortgage lenders then add on their profit markup to the index and the profit markup percentage, which is called the margin.

Here are some of the more popular ARM programs:

- *Traditional ARMs* – the interest rate starts out with a low rate to entice you to sign-up (called a teaser rate) then begins its slow or not-so-slow climb upward each month or whatever agreed upon time frame you selected.
- *Interest Only ARMs* – you only pay the interest each month for the specified time period you selected and when the time elapses you begin paying the additional principal and interest payment.
- *Option ARMs* – you get four options each month of what you want to pay.

    a) Minimum monthly payment
    b) Interest-only payment
    c) 30 Year payment
    d) 15 Year payment

It seems like a good option at first, but the biggest risk is that most people end up paying the minimum or interest only payment and end up owing more than the property is worth. This happens because the lenders just add what you are supposed to be paying to your loan balance. They then adjust your payments every year to reflect the new loan balance. This is called negative amortization. It is really just playing a game of Russian roulette in Mortgageville.

- *Hybrid ARMs* – these are usually shown as 3/1, 5/1, 7/1 or 10/1. This means they are fixed for 3, 5, 7 or 10 years, and then adjust every year after the specified period of time.

If you thinking of choosing an adjustable rate mortgage then you need to know the following before you sign:

- *Starting interest rate:* This is your initial interest rate.

- *Adjustment period*: Your option of having your rate change monthly, biannual or annual and if you choose this mortgage you should always choose annual.

- *Index*: The cost for your mortgage lender to borrow the money. You should choose a slow changing index life (COFI) because as your lenders index rate goes up, so does yours.

- *Life-of-the-loan cap*: This is the highest interest rate your mortgage will go up to.

- *Periodic cap*: This limits how much the interest can adjust in a one year period.

- *Low margin*: This is the mortgage lenders profit margin and may be around 2.75 percentage points.

- *Prepayment Penalty*: A penalty for paying your mortgage off early. Usually around six month's worth of mortgage payments. You should never use a mortgage that has a prepay penalty – why should you get penalized for paying off your mortgage sooner?

- *Negative amortization*: When you make the minimum monthly payment it is actually lower than what you really owe. The difference between the minimum payment and what a regular payment should be is added to your total mortgage at the end of the year. You could end up owing more than you borrowed when you make the minimum monthly payment.

- *Assumability*: You may be able to sign over your mortgage to your homebuyer when you sell your home – it is called an assumable mortgage when this happens.

Interest Rates

When buying a home the interest rate is one of the most important factors, so I will give you some inside tips and suggestions. You should always look at the three sides of an interest rate when borrowing money:

- **The base interest rate.** The interest rate the mortgage professional secured from the lender for your mortgage.

- **The Annual Percentage Rate (APR).** The total cost of your loan including the closing costs, which is divided over the number of years of your loan. (This number will be different than the base interest rate which does not have any fees or closing costs factored in)

- **The lifetime cost of the loan.** The big scary number that shows you how much you are paying back over the next thirty years.

Here is a chart to further illustrate the point of the impact of interest rates on your mortgage.

Monthly Payments for $250,000 (30 Year Fixed Rate Mortgage)	
This chart shows you how your monthly payment can change based on the interest rate. (taxes, insurance and other payments not included)	
5.0%	$1,342
5.5%	$1,419
6.0%	$1,498
6.5%	$1,580
7.0%	$1,663
7.5%	$1,748
8.0%	$1,834
8.5%	$1,922
9.0%	$2,011
9.5%	$2,102
10.0%	$2,193

So What is Better, Fixed Or Adjustable?

The best mortgage to use when buying a foreclosure depends on your goals and needs. Only you and your family can make the ultimate decision, but here is a chart to guide you in making your decision:

Mortgage Program Selection Guide	
You should get a fixed interest rate mortgage... (***Includes 50, 40, 30, 25, 20, 15 or 10 year term periods.)	If you: • Want stability • Want peace of mind • Are risk-adverse • Do not know if you will ever get a raise that is more than the rate of inflation • Do not ever want to move again • Have your ultimate dream home • Have a long term plan for the house
You should get an adjustable rate mortgage... (***Includes 1/1, 2/1, 3/1, 5/1, 7/1, 10/1, Option ARMs, Interest Only ARMs, Hybrid ARMs)	If you: • Plan on moving in the next three to five years • Make seasonal income that varies dramatically • Do not mind a little risk • Have significant savings • Bought a starter home knowing you will outgrow it quickly • Manage your finances well • Have a strong financial markets background and understand how financial markets operate.

The Truth About Points, Fees And Yield Spread

When obtaining a mortgage points, fees and yield spread are terms you should know and understand. They are lumped into three major categories:

- **Mortgage Points** – You may be offered to pay points to get a lower interest rate or you may be charged a point by the mortgage lender for originating your mortgage. If you are paying points to get a lower interest rate it is called discount points. Points are equal to 1% of your loan amount. So if your mortgage is $250,000 then one point costs $2,500.

- **Mortgage Fees** – Fees are the costs which you pay because you are getting a mortgage. You must be careful in this area because some mortgage lenders will really pile them on, but generally speaking, here are the major ones you should expect to pay:

  - *Appraisal*: Lenders require appraisals to determine the home value before they make a lending decision.

  - *Attorney Fee/Escrow Fee/Settlement Fee*: Every mortgage closing needs a third party to handle the closing and disperse funds.

  - *Credit Report*: Your lender will not make a decision without reviewing your credit reports. Make sure you receive a copy.

  - *Courier Fee*: In some cases there are several documents which are required to be shipped overnight.

  - *Flood Certification*: Your house must not be in a flood plain and to determine this you must pay a fee.

- *Processing Fee*: Every mortgage has a fair amount of paperwork which requires a gatekeeper for completing and submitting paperwork to lenders.
- *Recording Fee or Reconveyance Fee*: In order to make your sale final and legally binding your mortgage paperwork has to be documented at the courthouse.

- *Tax Service Fee*: Lenders always make sure that your taxes on the house are paid current before you close.

- *Title Insurance*: This one-time fee protects you against other people making a claim that they are the rightful owners of your home. Title insurance is required by law.

- *Title Review*: In some cases your attorney will charge a separate fee for reviewing all of the past records for your title.

- *Underwriting Fee* – Every lender charges an underwriting fee to perform all of the necessary evaluations before lending you money.

- **Yield Spread Premium** –This is basically an incentive program paid by your mortgage lender to your mortgage professional for either charging you a higher interest rate or qualifying you for a specific mortgage program. This is one area which has been under a lot of scrutiny in recent years because it has caused some loan officers to steer clients towards dangerous mortgage programs because of the profit in doing so. Be sure to ask your mortgage professional how many points will he or she be earning total on your mortgage and simply ask for a par rate.

The Best Mortgage Program To Use When Buying A Foreclosure Bargain

There is one mortgage program which allows all applicants to get a low fixed interest rate and take advantage of the best down payment assistance programs. In my experience, every foreclosure buyer who plans to *live* in the foreclosure home they purchase should work with a mortgage company that accepts both conventional mortgage and specializes in FHA (Federal Housing Administration) loans. The FHA is a government agency that insures residential mortgage loans for people who are interested in purchasing their first home – or even their second home after a specified period of time of non-ownership. An FHA loan is designed to help buyers who want to minimize their down payment to qualify for a conventional mortgage loan.

An FHA mortgage also helps people who have less than perfect credit build their credit and increase their FICO score. A higher FICO score helps you secure loans for vehicles, furniture, home improvement projects, and even credit cards. If you pay your mortgage on time every month, your credit score will improve drastically just within the first five years of paying your mortgage. If you are lucky enough to be able to pay off your home early, you will be able to enjoy the extra money for other things, such as a dream vacation, all without worrying about defaulting on your home.

The paperwork and components that you will need to get approved for an FHA mortgage is the same as with a conventional mortgage:

- W2's from the last two tax years
- Last two years of complete tax returns
- Paystubs
- Previous two months of bank statements
- Two years of stable job history
- Credit scores above 640
- At least 12-24 months of on-time rent payments
- 3.5 – 10% of purchase price for the down payment
- Basic forms verifying your identity, mortgage loan application and employment history

So, What Are My Choices?
When choosing a mortgage lender be sure to find out if you will have access to all of the area mortgage programs or just a few. In most cases your regular bank that holds your savings and checking account can only allow you to use their own programs. Their limited options may or may not work out in your favor.

In this next section I will cover the questions you should ask your mortgage professional about the mortgage loans they offer. I will also cover some of the mistakes many foreclosure buyers may make during the purchasing process, and help dispel some of the myths that surround FHA loans.

Q & A: FHA Mortgages

Once you have placed an offer on a home, placed an earnest money deposit on the house, the next step is to obtain financing for your home. As a foreclosure buyer, you should be aware of how this process works. These questions and answers will help educate you on the process and how this applies to an FHA loan:

- **What type of guidelines do I have to meet for an FHA loan?**
  Since FHA loans are considered the easiest mortgage loan to qualify for and the most flexible, the guidelines you need to meet are not that difficult.
  You must have:
  - At least two years of steady employment, preferably with the same employer.
  - Income over the last two years that has been steady or has increased.
  - Less than two thirty day late payments over the last two years, or a letter explaining the issues on the credit report to satisfy the FHA inquiry.
  - If you have filed for bankruptcy in the past, it must be

at least two years old with a good credit record since filing.

o A mortgage payment equals approximately 30% of your gross income which is based on the purchase price of the house, your other monthly bills, income, and current interest rates.

- **After I fill out the mortgage application, how long do I have wait for an answer?**
Getting an answer on whether or not you are accepted for the loan you applied for can take anywhere from 15 to 30 days. Some home transactions can take up to 60 days for a decision to be made. If you are required to provide the loan officer additional documentation – such as an explanation of items on your credit report – this could affect the time it takes to get an answer. The faster you provide the information, the faster you will get an answer. The lender reviewing your application will also be requesting an appraisal of the property, a copy of your credit report, verification of your employment information and banking records.

- **How much do I need for a down payment if I qualify for an FHA loan?**
Most loans require a down payment that equals approximately 3.5% of the purchasing price, but some applicants may qualify for a no down payment FHA loan. Your mortgage professional will be able to tell you if you need a down payment and how it can be paid or arranged. FHA will allow applicants to use money that is given to them from a family member or employer for their down payment.

- **What will the annual percentage rate on my loan be? Is it the same as the interest rate on my loan?**
We will answer the second question first. The annual percentage rate (APR) is not the same as the interest rate on your loan. The interest rate on your loan is the percentage you pay per so many dollars you borrow. This is the fee the lender charges you to borrow the money.

The APR is a value that reflects the actual cost of borrowing the money and it includes all of the fees that go with purchasing your home. Because each loan is different, your APR will be different than someone else's. There is no set number because the government uses a special formula to calculate this number. This number is determined by taking the amount of money you are borrowing and adding the closing costs on the loan and any other fees accumulated to the borrowing amount. All of the interest that you will be paying over the length of the loan – usually 30 years for an FHA loan – is added into the figure and it is then broken down into the rate, reflected as percentage.

Say you borrow $50,000 to pay for the home. Your closing costs are $700, and additional fees equal $2,000. Your APR will be determined how much interest is paid on $52,700 over 30 years and then broken down into a percentage.

- **What about the interest rate on my loan? Is it locked in place until I close or will it change?**
  The interest rate on your loan from first quote to final closing can change unless you submit a purchase and sales contract, complete loan application, and property appraisal. The interest rate will fluctuate with the market, and most mortgage lenders can no longer lock a rate into place until they have all three of these documents on file. If you want to get the lower rate then you should submit the items you are responsible for as soon as possible.

- **Will I get penalized if I pay off my mortgage loan before the end of the term?**
  Usually there is no prepayment penalty, but it is advised that you verify this information with your mortgage company after you have secured your loan to be sure. Each lender is a little different, so it is better to be cautious and assume nothing. It would be horrible to pay off your home to find out that you still owe the lender because of a prepayment penalty amount.

- **What could delay the approval of my mortgage loan?**
  There are many things that could delay your approval and most of them are usually beyond your control. You should discuss with your real estate agent and loan officer additional items that could delay the process.

But I Heard That FHA Mortgages Are...

Anyone who is interested in securing an FHA mortgage to buy a foreclosure property may hear a bunch of things about these types of loans that are not necessarily true. Difficult requirements to meet, needing perfect credit, having to have a large down payment...all of these things could make you nervous about buying a home. In this section I am going to debunk these myths so that you truly understand how easy it really is to secure one of these versatile loans and purchase a foreclosure.

- **Myth #1 – The government loans you the money for your home.**
  The FHA does not loan you money. The FHA guarantees the money that a bank, credit union, or other financial institution loans you. If you default on the mortgage, the FHA pays the lender the money you owe. This is one of the reasons why banks are able to loosen up their requirements for home loans. They are actually taking less of risk on you because of the government's promise to pay them.

- **Myth #2 – Your credit score does not matter when it comes to an FHA loan.**
  FHA bases their decision not only on your FICO or credit score, but on your actual credit history over the last two or more years. The state of your credit history is more important and they are looking for the way you make your payments – on time or late – and patterns of payment. The FHA will also take into consideration utility bill payments, rental history, phone bills, and other monthly bills that can help determine your credit worthiness.

- **Myth #3 – You get a better deal with an FHA loan.**
  This is not always true. Yes, this type of loan carries fewer risks for your lender and you get charged less by them, but they are not always the better deal. The FHA makes their money from the insurance that is paid to them. FHA loans are the better deal if you have low income or bad credit. If you have medium to good credit, you should shop around because you could get a better deal with a conventional mortgage loan.

- **Myth #4 – You will have to wait longer for an FHA loan approval.**
  This is a big, resounding NO. Thanks to the Internet that provides automated underwriting and paperless processing, it does not take the FHA any longer to approve a loan than it does a conventional loan. If you are under the care of an FHA educated loan officer, the process could even go faster as the paperwork and any documentation needed is submitted all at once, instead of piecemeal.

- **Myth #5 – There is a ton of extra paperwork associated with an FHA loan.**
  This is another big resounding NO. Conventional loans and FHA loans have pretty much the same amount of paperwork that needs to be filled out and submitted. The FHA loans do require a few different, extra documents that need to be filled out, but they are designed to protect you while you are going through the process of securing the loan. Plus, with the ability to print off most of the documents with your demographic information – address, phone number, income, etc. – already filled in, the most you will need to do is initial a few more pages.

- **Myth #6 – I am going to pay more for an FHA loan than a conventional one.**
  I am not sure how this particular myth got started, but the

interest rate that is used on a conventional loan is the same that is used on an FHA loan. Both are based on the current market factors and interest rates that are in force at the time of price locking. As a matter of fact, most of the time the FHA mortgage payment is less expensive than a conventional loan. Homebuyers with an FHA loan actually make out better because their FICO score is not used to base interest rates on. Even with the FHA insurance premium rolled into the loan, the monthly amount could be less.

- **Myth #7 – The FHA mortgage insurance is unaffordable.**
  Not really. Any loan in which 80% or more of the property value is financed must carry mortgage insurance, whether it is a conventional loan or an FHA loan. This is in place so that a portion of the loan is paid to the lender if the borrower defaults on their payments. The previous rule stated that all buyers had to pay 20% down in order to get a mortgage. This is no longer the case. FHA requires a prepayment of 1.5% in insurance. This is added to your loan. Additionally, .50% per year is also added and divided up over your payments. This is a total of 2%, which is 1 % lower than the rate being charged by conventional loans.

- **Myth #8 – The guidelines for an FHA loan are very restrictive.**
  Once again, the answer here is no. FHA loans are actually very easy on borrowers. They have a higher maximum loan amount and they do not require an income restriction, like Fannie Mae and Freddie Mac loans, two companies that specialize in conventional loans. Buyers with credit history issues will find an FHA loan easier to obtain. Plus, FHA loans allow underwriters to actually look at the loan application and use common sense techniques to help decide whether or not you can actually afford and pay your mortgage. FHA loans also allow for an easier refinance process. Therefore, if the interest rates should drop drastically, FHA allows borrowers to refinance for a lower monthly payment.

Applying For Your Mortgage

When you are meeting with your mortgage professional, you should come prepared. I have seen it take weeks for some couples to get their paperwork together for an appointment and I have seen other couples do it in minutes. Generally speaking, here is the information you want to bring to your appointment:

- W2's from the last two tax years
- Last two years of complete tax returns
- Two most recent paystubs
- Previous two months of bank statements
- Rent payment receipts for the last 12 months
- Proof of 3% – 10% of purchase price for the down payment
- Basic forms verifying your identity, mortgage loan application and employment history

Once your mortgage professional has this information in hand you will receive your prequalification letter and a Good Faith Estimate. The Good Faith Estimate is a form which gives you all fees and information about your mortgage. Keep in mind that it is an estimate, but it should still be within 10% of the final numbers for your mortgage.

The Four Factors of Getting Your Mortgage Approvals Fast And Easy

There are four major factors that will determine your mortgage approval and the interest rate you will be paying:

1. **Income** – Have you had continuous employment for the last twenty four months and if so, how much have you averaged per hour? Remember to keep your base salary separate from over-time and bonuses because lenders view those very differently because they are not stable and reliable enough to merit the same weight as salary.

- **High Income Earners** - Just because you make $150,000 or more per year does not mean you are not hourly. Take a look at your paystub and you will find that your employer graciously took the time to break it down for you.

- **Self-Employed** – All the hard work you and your tax professional put into minimizing your tax liability could really hurt you. Here is why: lenders look at your net income for the tax year, not your gross income. Meaning if your half a million dollar a year business deducted every possible penny you could and only showed you with a net of twenty five thousand dollars for the tax year, then that is all lenders can use to qualify you for a mortgage. A paltry twenty five thousand dollars. I know…I know, it is not right, but that is the way it is in Mortgageville.

2. **Credit** – Does your credit report reflect steady payment history and the ability to manage your finances, or does it show a person who rarely pays bills on time? Lenders want to see at least a 640 middle credit score.

3. **Loan-To-Value (LTV)** – Loan-to-value is the percentage you are borrowing compared to the value of the property. If the purchase price is $250,000 and you have $7,500 for a down payment and closing costs, then you are borrowing $242,500. That means that you have a 97% LTV.

   EXAMPLE:
   $250,000 purchase price - $7,500 down payment = $242,500

   $242,500 / $250,000 = .97 or 97% LTV

4. **Rental Payment History** – Can you prove you have been paying your rent on time the last twenty four months? This can be easily shown by receipts and check stubs. If not, then you are viewed as more of a credit risk.

Why You May Get A Different Interest Rate Than The Advertisement Says

Over the years there have been many times where homebuyers have come to my office upset because they were promised a 4.99% interest rate from another mortgage professional, who later could not give them that rate. When I dug a little deeper I discovered that the interest rate they "thought" they were getting was actually an advertisement in the newspaper and did not accurately reflect their true income, credit and overall risk level from a lender's perspective.

So here are some of the occasions in which you might find yourself getting a dramatically different interest rate than what you heard on the radio, saw on T.V., or read in the newspaper:

- **You chose a different mortgage type.** Many times lenders will put the most attractive rates that will result in a lower monthly payment. However, they neglect to mention that less than one percent of people qualify for these programs.

- **On paper you look risky.** There is no substitute for having good credit and consistent income. If you do not have either one, then you may have a good story to tell, but on paper you look risky.

- **You are borrowing almost what the house is worth (High LTV).** Since the days of one hundred percent financing are long gone, most buyers are seeking the mortgage program that requires the smallest down payment. However, smaller down payments create a higher LTV, which usually means higher interest rate. The only exception to this rule is if you are using an FHA mortgage, which I will discuss in-depth a little later.

- **Your loan cannot be resold on the secondary market.** Banks view mortgages as investments, so they will package ten or twenty mortgages together and sell them as an investment package to other banks. So if they have a group of ten thirty year fixed mortgages with six percent interest rates, they will expect a six percent return each year for thirty years. However, if you are viewed as risky, then your mortgage lender might not be able to sell your mortgage to other investors, so you represent more risk to them.

- **Your loan may or may not have points.** The mortgage rate you saw may have included paying one or two points. Therefore, if you stated you did not want to pay points to your mortgage professional then you may get a higher interest rate and points. Points are included in the interest rate in order to provide compensation to the mortgage professional. This is otherwise called yield spread premium.

Qualifying For A Super-Size Jumbo Mortgage

Here is a news flash for you in case you hadn't noticed. In many areas the price of a home is well above the old $417,000 conventional loan limits! This could potentially add another level of stress to foreclosure buyers who are preparing to jump into this part of the market. However, do not worry, because I have put together a quick guide to walk you through the differences and what to expect when you need a lot more than $417,000 to buy your home:

- **ABSOLUTELY use a mortgage broker.** Mortgage brokers are mortgage professionals who have access to hundreds of lenders. A mortgage broker will be able to shop almost every bank for you without you having to contact each bank personally and go through the application process.

- **Expect to pay a slightly higher interest rate.** You must be prepared to ignore those annoying advertisement commercials that promise you 4.99% interest rates on a million dollar mortgage. They are simply not true for jumbo mortgages.

- **Be prepared for additional time to close.** Lenders usually have more questions and need more careful market analysis when lending on luxury homes. They are not simply picking on you. It is because luxury homes usually take longer to sell.

- **You may be asked for additional income documentation.** This is not the time to play vague mystery person with rich relatives. Lenders want to know who, when, why and where your income comes from.

- **Your credit reports will be more closely scrutinized.** Due to the larger mortgage amount, any little blemish on your credit could become a blaring issue because you're trying to borrow a jumbo amount of money.

- **Be willing, ready and able to talk about where your money comes from and why you get paid the way you do.** It is very likely that if you are seriously considering a jumbo mortgage, then you make jumbo-like income. With that being said, it is even more important that you be open, honest and forthcoming about every source of income reflecting on your tax returns.

- **Get out the checkbook because the appraisal and home inspection will cost considerably more than average homes.** Be prepared to pay slightly higher prices for your real estate services because of the risk involved with doing a larger mortgage.

CHAPTER 15

Preparing For Your Closing

Your big day is finally here. All of the gathering paperwork, shuffling through inspection reports and weekends spent looking at houses has finally come to an end. It is now time to close on your foreclosure. There are some things which still need to be wrapped up the day before *and* day of the closing. In fact, regardless of how well your real estate team plans your home closing, there will undoubtedly be some "unwrapping" that gives you a surprise or two.

The Final Walk-Through

Taking one last look at your soon-to-be home before going to the closing is the most important task you can do next to actually signing the mortgage and ownership transfer paperwork. There are some real estate professionals who recommend doing a final walk-through five days prior to closing. My advice to you is to perform the final walk-through right before the closing is scheduled, because there are too many things which could go wrong in five days. However, if you walk-through the house immediately before going to the closing, then you know exactly how the house will look when you get the keys in two or three hours.

You will need to have your real estate agent, the seller's agent, purchase and sales agreement and seller's disclosure when doing your final walk-through. This way you can cross reference any of the information or observations you see with what was agreed upon. However, it is important to not over-analyze anything you see and exaggerate your observations in hope of getting a last minute deal. However, under no circumstance should you skip the final walk-through because it could cost you big-time.

"But I Don't Like Surprises..."

Tina was bubbling with happiness and joy over navigating the entire home buying process without one mishap. Compared to what she'd seen her two best friends go through, she counted herself lucky and blessed.

She'd done it by the book. She got the mortgage first. Found a real estate agent second. Then she found a gorgeous and beautifully maintained raised ranch, which she absolutely adored. Her offer was a tad bit under asking price and was immediately accepted.

It was not until she visited her new home after the closing that she noticed something very different. She was shocked. Her bathroom was wrecked.

It seems that the sellers had ripped out the bathroom fixtures, toilet and marble countertop! She could not believe it! They seemed like such a nice couple every single time she met with them. Why would they do this to her?

Tina immediately called her real estate agent and attorney. Both were amazed at the audacity of the sellers. Her attorney promptly called the sellers attorney to review the purchase and sales contract and sure enough, the sale of the house included all the bathroom fixtures, including countertops and toilets.

Tina was relieved that she was covered, but she was not prepared for the four months that it took to legally force the sellers to reimburse her for her expense of refinishing the bathroom. Every day she regretted not walking through the house one final time before the closing.

Last Minute To-Do List

These are the series of tasks which should be completed the last twenty four hours prior to closing:

- **Go over the final closing amount at least three times.** – Closing costs associated with the purchase of your home are comprised of all loan fees, which include prepaid points, title and homeowners insurance, taxes, down payments and recording fees. You will want to double check all numbers to make sure they are roughly what you were expecting to pay. Your estimated costs, which you receive a day or two before your scheduled closing should be comparable to the fees outlined on your Good Faith Estimate. You should have received your Good Faith Estimate within three days after you submitted your mortgage application. Keep in mind that your Good Faith Estimate is just an estimate of what your costs may be. There is no real way to determine, with a fair of amount of accuracy, what your closing costs will exactly be prior to the day before or day of your closing.

- **Make sure you have the appropriate payment method for closing costs.** – The payment method you are paying your closing costs with makes a big difference when it comes time to close. The seller's closing agent will not accept personal checks and will expect any needed money to either be paid by certified bank check or direct wiring of money into their account.

- **Go through the closing documents with a fine tooth comb and ask any questions you have.** – The most stressful experience in the world is having an entire roomful of people all staring at you because you have a last minute question which everyone knows should have been answered days or weeks ago. You can prevent this from happening by arriving at your closing a couple of hours early to go over everything with your attorney, mortgage professional and real estate agent. This allows you to make sure you have a complete and thorough understanding before you sign one document.

- **Come to closing prepared.** – Bring a recent and legible copy of a photo ID, as well as any receipts from any and all inspection reports you paid prior to closing. It is also a good idea to bring any contracts and agreements which might have exchanged hands during the transaction, such as purchase and sales agreement and seller's disclosure, etc.

The Closing Basics

The technical definition of a closing is a settlement or meeting which consists of simultaneous events which transfer your money to the seller in exchange of ownership of the home. The normal everyday explanation is the closing is when you sign all the mortgage and homeownership paperwork and get the keys. Behind the scenes your lender is most likely verifying last minute information to make sure you did not suddenly quit your job or take on more monthly debt. In order to give you a better idea of how your closing will go, let's look at the three major parts of your closing:

- **The time of your closing** - You should have requested your exact or approximate closing date in your purchase and sales agreement. The date can change depending on your mortgage approval status or the seller needing additional time to clear title and such issues. However, the date on the purchase and sales agreement is the legally binding date which both parties can hold the other liable for. By the way, do not ever set the date of your closing to be on a weekend, because if you have an issue with any important documents the lender will be closed until the following Monday.

- **The location of your closing** - The closing will most likely be held at the seller's attorney's office. However, it can be at your attorney's office, depending on what is specified in the purchase and sales agreement.

- **Who should attend the closing** – Obviously you will be there, but you should also see your real estate agent, mortgage professional and attorney. The seller, their closing agent and real estate agent should also be present. Do not be intimidated by the amount of people at your closing. Your point of view should be, the more the merrier. After all, if something goes wrong you want all the people who can fix the problem to be present.

At The Closing

At long last the closing day is here. No matter when the closing is scheduled, plan on taking the entire day off from work to do any last minute running around. I have seen closings completed in one hour, and I have seen all day marathons which take several hours, and then some. The biggest difference in the length of closing time ultimately depends on you having read the documents in advance with your attorney. For whatever reason, if you have neglected to read your paperwork prior to closing, then be prepared to have to ask a ton of questions, which will dramatically slow down your closing.

"Oh My Goodness...Something *Else* Popped Up"
There has not been one closing I have attended over the years which has not had at least one last-minute surprise. It comes with the territory. I have had many types of last-minute challenges for my clients in past years. Things like old collection accounts show up on credit reports and paperwork gets lost. You will be happy to know that every single one of those closings was able to be completed. No matter what happens during your home buying process, stay positive and optimistic. It all works out in the end.

Even if you have prepared for the closing as recommended, you may still have additional questions, so don't hesitate to ask them at any point during the closing. However, keep in mind that you should be prepared to get a few annoying glances and irritated looks from the seller if they felt like you did not do your homework in advance of the closing that you have known about for two or three months.

Where is Your Homework?
You will be happy to know that you have the right to review your closing paperwork at least 24-48 hours before closing. This is the perfect time to review all of the numbers to make sure you're not being taken advantage of. You will also want to check to make sure the interest rate is fixed and that the name on the title is exactly how you want it.

Your closing is comprised of two major sections: mortgage paperwork and property ownership transfer paperwork.

Part One: The Mortgage Paperwork

The first part of your closing documents will focus on the financing side of things. The reason for this is simple; if there is no mortgage, then there is no transfer of property ownership. Also, keep in mind that you are buying a house for a certain amount, but when you add in the closing costs and fees, your total dollar amount for buying your home is usually several thousands of dollars more than the initial purchase price. Don't get too worried, because it is expected and normal for this to happen. Here are the documents you will see at your closing:

- **Promissory Note** – This is your agreement stating you are borrowing a specific amount of money and guarantee you will pay it back as agreed upon on the form.

- **Mortgage Deed** – This is a lien placed on your property which gives the lender the right to foreclose on your house for non-payment of the mortgage.

- **Truth-In-Lending (Regulation Z) Disclosures** – This gives you all the payments you will be making on your mortgage, your interest rates and the total lifetime amount of how much you are borrowing.

- **HUD-1 Settlement Statement** – This form itemizes every penny you will be paying in connection with your mortgage. It lists every fee such as insurance premiums, attorney and lender fees, down payment amount, etc.

- **Monthly Payment Coupon** - This will be your first payment statement that will let you know what to expect to pay each month and who to mail it to.

Part Two: The Property Ownership Transfer Paperwork

After the financing is taken care of, then it is time to transfer the property ownership to you. As expected there will be forms to sign, but there will also be paperwork such as certificates that will simply be handed over to you. Here is a list of some of the documents you should expect to see:

- **Warranty Deed** – This is the document that notifies everyone that the seller is transferring ownership of the property to you. When this document is recorded at the town or city hall it makes the transaction legally binding. It is important to note that it is when the documents are recorded that it is official, and NOT when it is signed.

- **Bill of Sale** – This covers all of the property and possessions which you are buying when you take over the property.

- **Affidavit of Title** – This is the seller's sworn statement that the title is in good condition and they have the legal right to sell the property to you as the owner.

- **ALTA Statement** - This is the American Land Title Association statement which gives the status of the property's title to allow you to purchase title insurance. This insurance protects you against outside claims to your home title after the purchase.

After signing all of the documents, be sure to get your keys and exchange contact information with the seller. There will be times when you will want to call them to ask about some of the nuances of your new home that only someone who has lived there will know. Be sure to check your purchase and sales agreement to see when you have legal right to take "possession" and move into your home.

Even though you have the keys, do not just assume that it is the closing date. Verify it against the date on your purchase and sales agreement. Also, be sure to know when the deed will be recorded because that will be the specific time that your purchase will be legally recognized by the town or city in which you bought your home.

IMPORTANT REAL ESTATE TERMS

Adjustable Rate Mortgage (ARM): Mortgage loans under which the interest rate is periodically adjusted to more closely coincide are agreed to at the inception of the loan.

Alternative Documentation: The use of pay stubs, W-2 forms, and bank statements in lieu of Verifications of Employment (VOE) and Verifications of Deposit (VOD) to qualify a borrower for a mortgage.

Amortization: The systematic and continuous payment of an obligation through installments until the debt has been paid in full.

Annual Percentage Rate (APR): A term used in the Truth-in-Lending Act to present the percentage relationship of the total finance charge to the amount of the loan. The APR reflects the cost of the mortgage loan as a yearly rate. It could be higher than the interest rate stated on the Note because it includes, in addition to the interest rate, loan discount points, miscellaneous fees and mortgage insurance.

Appraisal: A report made by a qualified person setting forth an opinion or estimate of property value. (Appraisal also refers to the process through which a conclusion on property value is derived.)

Appraisal Amount or Appraised Value: The fair market value of a home determined by an independent appraisal. The appraisal uses local real estate market sales activity as a major basis for valuation.

Appreciation: An increase in the value of a property due to market conditions or other causes. The opposite is depreciation.

Balloon Mortgage: A fixed-rate mortgage for a set number of years, and then must be paid off in full in a single "balloon" payment. Balloon loans are popular with borrowers expecting to sell or refinance their property within a definite period of time.

Bankruptcy: Legal relief from the payment of all debts after the surrender of all assets to a court-appointed trustee. Assets are distributed to creditors as full satisfaction of debts, with certain priorities and exemptions. A person, firm or corporation may declare bankruptcy under one of several chapters of the U. S. Bankruptcy Code: Chapter 7 covers liquidation of the debtor's assets; Chapter 11 covers reorganization of bankrupt businesses; Chapter 13 covers payment of debts by individuals through a bankruptcy plan.

Cap: The limit placed on adjustments that can be made to the interest rate or payments, such as the annual cap on an adjustable rate loan (ARM) or the cap on a rate over the life of the loan.

Cash-out Refinance: To refinance the mortgage on a property for more than the principal owed. This allows the borrower to get cash from the equity in their home. Loan products may vary on how much can be borrowed on a cash-out refinance.

Certified Mortgage Specialist (CMS): The Certified Mortgage Specialist is the professional sales associate who communicates the needs of the agent and borrower to the operation team.

Client Coordinator (CC): The Client Coordinator sets the tone throughout the application process and ensures that each customer is kept informed of all needs and status through clear and concise communication.

Closer: The person who coordinates the closing time with the Client Coordinator and reviews and prepares the necessary closing documents.

Closing: Also known as settlement, the finalization of the process of purchasing or refinancing real estate. The closing includes the delivery of a Deed, the signing of Notes and the disbursement of funds.

Closing Costs: These are costs that are due at closing, in addition to the purchase price of the property. These costs normally include, but are not limited to, origination fees, discount points, attorney's fees, costs for title insurance, surveys, recording documents, and prepayment of real estate taxes and insurance premiums held by the lender. Sometimes the seller will help the borrower pay some of these costs.

Closing Statement: An accounting of the debits and credits incurred at closing. All FHA, VA and Conventional financing loans use a Uniform Closing or Settlement Statement commonly referred to as the HUD-1.

Co-Borrower: A party who signs the mortgage note along with the primary borrower, and who also shares title to the subject real estate.

Collateral: Property pledged as security for a debt. For example, real estate that secures a mortgage. Collateral can be repossessed if the loan is not repaid.

Combined Loan To Value (CLTV): The mathematical relationship between the total of all loan amounts (first mortgage plus subordinate liens) and the value of the subject property.

Community Reinvestment Act (CRA): This act requires financial institutions to meet the credit needs of their community, including low and moderate-income sections of the local community. It also requires banks to make reports concerning their investment in the areas where they do business.

Condominium: A form of property ownership in which the homeowner holds title to an individual dwelling unit, an undivided interest in common areas of a multi-unit project, and sometimes the exclusive use of certain limited common areas. All condominiums must meet certain investor requirements.

Conforming Loan: A loan with a mortgage amount that does not exceed that which is eligible for purchase by FNMA or FHLMC. All loans are considered as conforming or non-conforming, also known as jumbo.

Conventional Loan: A mortgage loan not insured or guaranteed by the federal government.

Conversion Option: Options to convert an adjustable rate mortgage or balloon loan to a fixed rate mortgage under specified conditions.

Co-Signer: A party who signs the mortgage note along with the borrower, but who does not own or have any interest in the title to the property.

Creditor: A person to whom debt is owed by another person who is the "debtor".

Credit Rating: A rating given a person or company to establish credit-worthiness based upon present financial conditions, experience and past credit history.

Credit Report: A document completed by a credit-reporting agency providing information about the buyer's credit cards, previous mortgage history, bank loans and public records dealing with financial matters.

Deal Structure: An Underwriters review of certain aspects of a loan application that do not meet standard guidelines.

Debt to Income Ratio: Compares the amount of monthly income to the amount the borrower will owe each month in house payment (PITI) plus other debts. The other debts may include but not limited to car payment, credit cards, alimony, child support, and personal loans. This ratio is commonly used to see if the borrower has the capacity to repay the debt.

Deed of Trust: A legal document that conveys title to real estate to a disinterested third party (trustee) who holds the title until the owner of the property has repaid the debt. In states where it is used, a Deed of Trust accomplishes essentially the same purpose as a Mortgage.

Default: Failure to comply with the terms of any agreement. In real estate this is generally used in connection with a mortgage obligation to refer to the failure to comply with the terms of the Promissory Note. Most often this default is a failure to make payments. However, there are other means by which a borrower may default, such as the failure to pay real estate taxes.

Depreciation: A decline in the value of property. The opposite of appreciation.

Discount Points: A percentage of the loan amount which is charged or credited by the lender upon making a mortgage loan. Loans that are made at the present market rate, with no points, are considered to be made at "par." Because of the lender's ability to charge or credit points on an individual loan, the lender is able to tailor a loan program and interest rate to fit the needs of each individual borrower. Discount points can be negotiated in the Purchase Contract to be paid by either the seller or the borrower.

Each point equals 1% of the mortgage loan. For example, a charge of 1 point on a $50,000 loan would result in a charge of $500; 1/2 point would be $250 ($50,000 x .50%).

Down Payment: The part of the purchase price which the buyer pays in cash and does not finance with a mortgage.

Earnest Money: Deposit made by a purchaser of real estate as evidence of good faith.

Equal Credit Opportunity Act (ECOA): Also known as Regulation B. A federal law that prohibits a lender from discriminating in mortgage lending on the basis of race, color, religion, national origin, sex, marital status, age, income derived from public assistance programs, or previous exercise of Consumer Credit Protection Act rights.

Equity: The difference between the current market value of a property and the principal balance of all outstanding loans.

Escrow Account: An account held by the lending institution to which the borrower pays monthly installments for property taxes, insurance, and special assessments, and from which the lender disburses these sums as they become due.

Fair Credit Reporting Act: Regulated the collection and distribution of information by the consumer credit reporting industry. It also affects how financial institutions collect and convey credit information about loan applicants or borrowers.

Fair Housing Act: Prohibits the denial or variance of the terms of real estate related transactions based on race, color, religion, sex, national origin, disability, or familiar status of the credit applicant. Real estate related transactions include a mortgage, home improvement, or other loans secured by a dwelling.

Federal Home Loan Mortgage Corporation (FHLMC): Also known as Freddie Mac. A publicly owned corporation created by Congress to support the secondary mortgage market. It purchases and sells conventional residential mortgages as well as residential mortgages insured by the Federal Housing Administration (FHA) or guaranteed by the Veterans Administration (VA).

Federal National Mortgage Association (FNMA): Also known as Fannie Mae. A privately owned corporation to support the secondary mortgage market. It adds liquidity to the mortgage market by investing in home loans through the country.

FICO Score: A credit score given to a person that establishes creditworthiness based on present financial conditions, experience and past credit history.

Finance Charge: The cost of credit as a dollar amount (i.e. total amount of interest and specific other loan charges to be paid over the term of the loan and other loan charges to be paid by the borrower at closing). Loan charges include origination fees, discount points, mortgage insurance, and other applicable charges. If the seller pays any of these charges, they cannot be included in the finance charge.

Financial Statement: A summary of facts showing an individual's or company's financial condition. For individuals, it states their assets and liabilities as of a given date. For a company it should include a Profit and Loss Statement (P&L) for a certain period of time and balance sheet, stating assets and liabilities as of a given date.

First Mortgage: A real estate loan that creates a primary lien against real property.

First Rate Adjustment -- First rate adjustment after: In association with an Adjustable Rate Mortgage loan, this is the number of months after which the loan has closed when the first interest rate adjustment will occur.

First Rate Adjustment -- Maximum rate decrease: In association with an Adjustable Rate Mortgage loan, this is the most the interest rate can decrease during the first adjustment period.

First Rate Adjustment -- Maximum rate increase: In association with an Adjustable Rate Mortgage loan, this is the most the interest rate can increase during the first adjustment period.

Fixed Rate Mortgage: The type of loan where the interest rate will not change for the entire term of the loan.

Floating: The term used when a purchaser elects not to lock-in an interest rate at the time of application.

Flood Insurance: Insurance that compensates for direct physical damages by or from flood to the insured property subject to the terms, provisions, conditions and losses not covered provision of the policy. It is required for mortgages on properties located in federally designated flood areas.

Good Faith Estimate (GFE): An estimate of settlement charges paid by the borrower at closing. The Real Estate Settlement Procedures Act (RESPA) requires a Good Faith Estimate of settlement charges be provided to the borrower.

Gift Letter: A letter or affidavit that indicates that part of a borrower's down payment is supplied by relatives or friends in the form of a gift and that the gift does not have to be repaid.

Gross Income: A person's income before deductions for income taxation.

Hazard Insurance: Insurance against losses caused by perils which are commonly covered in policies described as a "Homeowner Policy".

Home Maintenance: Costs associated with maintaining a home. This may include, but not limited to, general repairs, replacement or repair of furnace, air conditioning, roof, plumbing and electrical systems.

Home Mortgage Disclosure Act (HMDA): Also known as Regulation C. The purpose of HMDA is to provide disclosure of mortgage lending application activity (home purchase or improvement) to regulators and the public. Information is collected on each application, and is recorded on a log that is compiled to produce a report on application activity by geographic designation (census tract).

Homeowners Association (HOA): A non-profit corporation or association that manages common areas and services of a Condominium or Planned Unit Development (PUD).

Homeowners Insurance: Insurance that covers damage to the insured's' residence and liability claims made against the insured subject to the policy terms, conditions, provisions, losses not insured provision and exclusions.

Housing Expense Ratio: Ratio used to determine the borrowers capacity to repay a home loan. The ratio compares monthly income to the house payment (Principal, Interest, Taxes and Insurance).

Index: In connection with ARM loans, the external measurement used by a Lender to determine future changes which are to occur to an adjustable loan program. These will typically be published rates that are independent of the Lender's control, such as a Treasury Bill.

Initial Interest Rate: The beginning interest rate at the start of an adjustable rate mortgage (ARM). It may be lower than the fully indexed rate or "going market rate" and it will remain constant until it is adjusted up or down on the adjustment date.

Interest: The amount paid by a borrower to a lender for the use of the lender's money for a certain period of time. The amount paid by a bank on some deposit accounts.

Interest Income: The potential income from funds which would have been used for the down payment, closing costs, and any difference (increase) between monthly rental payment and monthly mortgage payment.

Interest Rate: The percentage of an amount of money that is paid for its use for a specific time; usually expressed as an annual percentage.

Judgment: Decree of a court declaring that one individual is indebted to another and fixing the amount of such indebtedness.

Jumbo Loan: A loan above the limit set by the Federal National Mortgage Association (Fannie Mae) and the Federal Home Loan

Mortgage Corporation (Freddie Mac). Also referred to as a non-conforming loan.

Late Charge: An additional charge a borrower is required to pay as a penalty for failure to pay a regular mortgage loan installment when due; a penalty for a delinquent payment.

Lien: A legal claim against a property that must be paid off when the property is sold. A lien is created when you borrow money and use your home as collateral for the loan.

Life of Loan -- Maximum rate decrease: In association with an Adjustable Rate Mortgage loan, this is the most the interest can decrease over the life of the mortgage loan.

Life of Loan -- Maximum rate increase: In association with an Adjustable Rate Mortgage loan, this is the most the interest can increase over the life of the mortgage loan.

Loan Application: A source of information on which the lender bases a decision to make or not make a loan; defines the terms of the loan contract, gives the names of the borrower(s), place of employment, salary, bank accounts, credit references, real estate owned, and describes the property to be mortgaged.

Loan Balance: The amount of unpaid principal balance that is remaining and owed by the borrower.

Loan Term: Number of years a loan is amortized. Mortgage loan terms are generally 15, 20, or 30 years.

Loan-to-Value (LTV): The ratio of the total amount borrowed on a mortgage against a property, compared to the appraised value of the property. An LTV ratio of 90 means that the borrower is borrowing 90% of the value of the property and paying 10% as a down payment. For purchases, the value of the property is the lesser of the purchase price or the appraised value. For refinances the value is determined by an appraisal.

Loan-to-Value Ratio: The ratio, expressed as a percentage, of the amount of the loan (numerator) to the value or selling price of real property (denominator). For example, if you have an $80,000 1st mortgage on a home with an appraised value of $100,000, the LTV is 80% ($80,000 / $100,000 = 80%).

Lock-In: A written agreement between the lender and borrower for a specified period of time in which the lender will hold a specific interest rate, origination and/or discount point(s).

Margin: Under the terms of an adjustable rate mortgage (ARM), the margin is a set adjustment to the index. The particular loan product determines the amount of the margin.

Median Income: The middle income level. Half of the incomes would be higher than the median income and half of the incomes would be below the median income. This is not to be confused with an average income.

Mortgage: The written instrument used to pledge a title to real estate as security for repayment of a Promissory Note.

Mortgage Insurance: Insurance written in connection with a mortgage loan that indemnifies the lender in the event of borrower default. In connection with conventional loan transactions, this insurance is commonly referred to as Private Mortgage Insurance (PMI).

Mortgage Note: A written promise to pay a sum of money at a stated interest rate during a specified term. It is typically secured by a mortgage.

Mortgage Servicing: Controlling the necessary duties of a mortgagee, such as collecting payments, releasing the lien upon payment in full, foreclosing if in default, and making sure the taxes are paid, insurance is in force, etc. The lender or a company acting for the lender, for a servicing fee, may do servicing. (Also called Loan Servicing.)

Mortgagee: The institution, group, or individual that lends money on the security of pledged real estate; the association, the lender.

Mortgagee Clause: This is the clause that is typically used for hazard insurance and flood insurance. For loans originated by the State Farm Bank it will read: State Farm Bank, F.S.B., Its Successor and/or Assigns, P.O. Box 2583, Ft. Wayne, IN 46801-2583.

Mortgagor: The owner of real estate who pledges his property as security for the repayment of a debt; the borrower.

Net Income: The difference between effective gross income and expenses, including taxes and insurance. The term is qualified as net income before depreciation and debt.

Non-Conforming: A loan with a mortgage amount that exceeds that which is eligible for purchase by FNMA or FHLMC. All other loans above this amount are considered to be non-conforming or jumbo loans.

Non-Owner-Occupied Property: Property purchased by a borrower not for a primary residence but as an investment with the intent of generating rental income, tax benefits, and profitable resale.

Note: A written promise by one party to pay a specific sum of money to a second party under conditions agreed upon mutually. Also called a "Promissory Note."

Note Rate: The interest rate on the mortgage loan.

Origination Fee: A fee paid to a lender for processing a loan application; it is stated as a percentage of the mortgage amount.

Origination Process: Process in which a lender solicits business, gathers required information and commits to loan money for the purchase of real estate.

Owner-Occupied Property: The borrower or a member of the immediate family lives in the property as a primary residence.

PITI: Term commonly used to refer to a mortgage loan payment. Acronym stands for Principal, Interest, Taxes, and Insurance.

PITI Ratio: Compares the amount of the monthly income to the amount the borrower will owe each month in principal, interest, real estate tax and insurance on a mortgage. Lenders use it in deciding whether to give the borrower a loan. Also called "income-to-debt" ratio.

Planned Unit Development (PUD): A housing project that may consist of any combination of homes (one-family to four-family), condominiums, and various other styles. In a PUD, often the individual unit and the land upon which it sits are owned by the unit/homeowner; however, the homeowner's association owns common facilities.

Pre-Approval: A process in which a customer provides appropriate information on income, debts and assets that will be used to make a credit only loan decision. The customer typically has not identified a property to be purchased; however, a specific sales price and loan amount are used to make a loan decision. (The sales price and loan amount are based on customer assumptions)

Pre-Qualification: A process designed to assist a customer in determining a maximum sales price, loan amount and PITI payment they are qualified for. A pre-qualification is not considered a loan approval. A customer would provide basic information (income, debts, assets) to be used to determine the maximum sales price, etc.

Prepaid Expenses or Prepaids: The term used to describe the funds the Lender requires to be deposited to establish the escrow account for taxes and insurance at the time of closing (also refers to Prepaid Interest).

Prepaid Interest: Interest that the borrower pays the lender before it becomes due.

Prepayment: A loan repayment made in advance of its contractual due date.

Prepayment Penalty: A penalty under a Note, Mortgage or Deed of Trust imposed when the loan is paid before its maturity date.

Principal and Interest: Two components of a monthly mortgage payment. Principal refers to the portion of the monthly payment that reduces the remaining balance for the mortgage. Interest is the fee charged for borrowing money.

Principal Balance: The outstanding balance of a mortgage, not counting interest.

Principal, Interest, Real Estate Tax, Insurance Payment: The total mortgage payment which includes principal, interest, taxes and insurance.

Private Mortgage Insurance (PMI): Insurance against a loss by a lender in the event of default by a borrower (mortgagor). A private insurance company issues this insurance. The premium is paid by the borrower and is included in the mortgage payment.

Processing: Gathering the loan application and all required supporting documents (including the property appraisal, credit report, credit history, and income and expenses) so that a lender can consider the borrower for a loan.

Promissory Note: A document in which the borrower promises to pay a stated amount on a specific date. The note normally states the name of the lender, the terms of payment and any interest rate.

Property Taxes: Taxes assessed on real estate. Property taxes are based on valuations by local and or state governments.

Purchase Agreement: A written agreement between a buyer and seller of real property that states the price and terms of the sale.

Purchase Price: The total amount paid for a home.

Qualifying Income Ratios: Income analysis used by lenders in deciding whether or not to offer the borrower a loan. One type of analysis compares only the amount of the proposed monthly mortgage payment to the monthly income. Another compares the amount of the total monthly payments (for example car, credit card and proposed mortgage payments) to the monthly income.

Rate Index: An index used to adjust the interest rate of an adjustable mortgage loan.

Real Estate Appreciation Rate: Percentage increase in the value of real estate, expressed at an annual rate.

Real Estate Settlement Procedures Act (RESPA): A consumer protection law that requires, among other things, lenders to give borrowers advance notice of closing costs.

Realtor: A person licensed to negotiate and transact the sale of real estate on behalf of the property owner. A real estate broker or associate must hold active membership in a real estate board affiliated with the National Association of Realtors.

Recording Fee: The amount paid to the recorder's office in order to make a document a matter of public record.

Regulation Z: Federal Reserve regulation issued under the Truth-in-Lending Act, which, among other things, requires that a credit purchaser be advised in writing of all costs connected with the credit portion of the loan.

Rental Payment: A payment made to use another's property. The amount of the rent is determined in a contract and is typically paid monthly.

Renters Insurance: Insurance against perils which are commonly covered in policies described as a "Renters Policy".

Repayment: The payment of a mortgage loan over a period of time, established when the loan is originated.

Rescind: To avoid or cancel in such a way as to treat the contract or other object of the rescission as if it never existed.

Sales Contract: A written agreement between parties stating all terms and conditions of a sale.

Savings Rate: The interest rate a person expects to earn on a savings account or investment account.

Secondary Market: An informal market where existing mortgages are bought and sold. It is the traditional aftermarket for mortgage loans that brings together lenders that sell mortgages with lenders, investors and agencies that buy mortgages.

Seller Contribution: The seller may be paying some or all of the borrower's cost. The amount of the contribution has limitations.

Selling Costs: The costs incurred in selling a home. This could include Realtor expenses and other miscellaneous expenses such as painting or minor repairs to prepare the home for sale.

Servicing: All the management and operational procedures that the mortgage company handles for the life of the loan, up through foreclosure if necessary, including: collecting the mortgage payments, ensuring that the taxes and insurance charges are paid promptly, and sending an annual report on the mortgage and escrow accounts.

Servicing Released: A stipulation in the agreement for the sale of mortgages in which the Lender is not responsible for servicing the loan.

Servicing Retained: A loan sale in which the original lender's servicing department continues to service the loan after the sale to a secondary institution or investor.

Settlement Statement: Also referred to as a HUD-1 Settlement Statement. The complete breakdown of costs involved in the real estate transaction for both the seller and buyer.

Single-Family Attached Home: A single-family dwelling that is attached to other single-family dwellings.

Single-Family Detached Home: A freestanding dwelling for a single family

Survey: A measurement of land, prepared by a registered land surveyor, showing the location of the land with reference to known points, its dimensions and the location and dimensions of any improvements.

Subordinate Financing: An additional lien against the real estate securing borrower's first mortgage. This lien takes second priority to the first mortgage.

Subsequent Rate Adjustment -- Maximum rate decrease: In association with an Adjustable Rate Mortgage loan, this is the most the interest rate can decrease when it is scheduled for reevaluation and possible adjustment.

Subsequent Rate Adjustment -- Maximum rate increase: In association with an Adjustable Rate Mortgage loan, this is the most the interest rate can increase when it is scheduled for reevaluation and possible adjustment.

Subsequent Rate Adjustment -- Next ARM Adjustment Date: In association with an Adjustable Rate Mortgage loan, this is the date scheduled for the next reevaluation and possible adjustment.

Subsequent Rate Adjustment -- Rate Change Frequency: In association with an Adjustable Rate Mortgage loan, this is the frequency in which possible adjustments may be made to the interest rate amount for Adjustable Rate Mortgages after the initial adjustment.

Tax Rates: Tax levied by the federal government and some states based on a person's income. Federal income tax rates vary depending on a person's adjusted gross income.

Tax Savings: The amount saved on taxes by itemizing deductions on income tax returns.

Title: The evidence to the right to or ownership in property. In the case of real estate, the documentary evidence of ownership is the title deed, which specifies in whom the legal state is vested and the history of ownership and transfers. Title may be acquired through purchase, inheritance, devise, gift or through the foreclosure of a mortgage.

Title Insurance Policy: A contract by which the insurer, usually a title company, indicates who has legal title and agrees to pay the insured a specific amount of any loss caused by clouds, claims or defects of title to real estate, which the insured has an interest as owner, mortgagee or otherwise.

(a) Owner's Title Policy: Usually issued to the landowner himself. The owner's title insurance policy is bought and paid for only once and then continues in force without any further payment. Owner's Title Insurance policies are not assignable.

(b) Mortgagee's Title Policy: Issued to the mortgagee and terminates when the mortgage debt is paid. In the event of foreclosure, or if the mortgagee acquires title from the mortgagor in lieu of foreclosure, the policy continues in force, giving continued protection against any defects of title which existed at, or prior to, the date of the policy.

Treasury Bills: Interest bearing U.S. Government obligations sold at a weekly sale. The change in interest rates paid on these obligations is frequently used as the Rate Index for Adjustable Mortgage Loans.

Truth in Lending (TIL): The name given to the federal statutes and regulations (Regulation Z) which are designed primarily to insure that prospective Borrowers of credit received credit and cost information before concluding a loan transaction.

Underwriting (Mortgage Loans): The process of evaluating a loan application to determine the risk involved for the lender. It involves an analysis of the borrower's creditworthiness and the quality of the property itself.

Verification of Deposit (VOD): Form used in mortgage lending to verify the deposits or assets of a prospective borrower when monthly statements are unavailable or unusable.

Verification of Employment (VOE): Form used in mortgage lending to verify the employment and income of a prospective borrower when pay stubs and W2 forms are unavailable or unusable.

Verification of Mortgage (VOM): Form used in mortgage lending to verify the existing mortgage balance, monthly payments and late payments, if any.

Verification of Rent: Form used in mortgage lending to verify monthly rents paid and late payments, if any.

www.ingramcontent.com/pod-product-compliance
Lightning Source LLC
Chambersburg PA
CBHW051520170526
45165CB00002B/547